D1708464

good garden magic

good garden magic

back-to-basics
Gardening
in a flash

celia toler

MQP

Published by **MQ Publications Limited**
12 The Ivories
6–8 Northampton Street
London N1 2HY
Tel: +44 (0)20 7359 2244
Fax: +44 (0)20 7359 1616
email: mail@mqpublications.com
website: www.mqpublications.com

Copyright © 2003 MQ Publications Limited
Text copyright © 2003 Celia Toler
ILLUSTRATION: **gerardgraphics.co.uk**
DESIGN: **balley design associates**

ISBN: 1 84072 450 1

10 9 8 7 6 5 4 3 2 1

All rights reserved. No part of this publication may be
reproduced or transmitted in any form or by any
means, electronic and mechanical, including photocopy,
recording, or any information storage and retrieval
system now known or to be invented without
permission in writing from the publishers.

Printed and bound in China

Contents

Introduction

This is not a book of opinions about what I think you should be growing, but instead, an enthusiastic book to help you to understand the plants you choose to grow—a straightforward guide on how to garden that explains the magic without dispelling it. A garden combines the miracle of growth with the visual pleasures of leaf, flower, and berry while providing shelter and food for wildlife—bees, butterflies, and birds that brighten our lives and act as a balm for the spirit battered by modern life.

Good Garden Magic begins where all good gardening begins: with the cultivation of the soil. It explains how to grow healthy plants using traditional and organic methods. This avoids using chemical fertilizers or pesticides since these are increasingly shown to damage the structure of the soil and to be bad for the environment. Organic fertilizers improve the soil, which promotes stronger plants and in turn means they are less susceptible to pests.

Next come the plants themselves, from small bulbs to giant trees, with a section devoted to edible plants. Discover the magic of serving up your own beans or tomatoes and of pears or cherries eaten fresh from the tree. Finally comes the care of spaces within a garden, such as the lawn, the pond, and containers. And in every chapter the Green Witch interjects her own brand of tips and advice.

Gardening is not for the faint-hearted, not only because of the physical work, but also because you will need a strong stomach for some of the more potent mixtures! There are also disappointments when plants fail or are massacred before they have had a chance to get going. These are the realities of gardening. But where one plant fails there is always another that survives. In the end, there is nothing quite like the feeling of self-sufficiency, achievement, and integration wit our world that caring for a garden through wind, rain, and sunshine can give.

Good gardening!—and watch the magic untold.

The Soil and the Seed

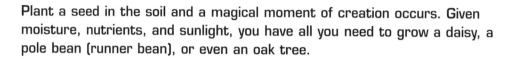

Plant a seed in the soil and a magical moment of creation occurs. Given moisture, nutrients, and sunlight, you have all you need to grow a daisy, a pole bean (runner bean), or even an oak tree.

The soil, rich in micro-organisms, is the basis of all our gardens, so whether you have extensive landscaped grounds or a window box, it makes sense to maintain and improve the soil as much as possible. Plants get what they require from the soil, but the food in chemical fertilizers is like a diet of vitamin pills without the fibre that keeps our own systems healthy. Far better to feed the soil rather than the plant. As well as providing a balance of nutrients that promote flower, vegetable and fruit production, organic composts improve soil structure and provide a healthy environment for plants. Gardening is not a precise science, but there are basic techniques that hold true for all plants.

The magic of plants

Plants are life. They provide sustenance, either directly or through being eaten by other animals, and while we inhale oxygen and exhale carbon dioxide, plants absorb carbon dioxide and return oxygen to the atmosphere. More plants mean more oxygen and by taking up carbon dioxide, plants lessen the effect this gas has on global warming through the greenhouse effect. This is why parks and forests are often referred to as the planet's lungs.

Photosynthesis

One of the greatest pieces of magic is the transformation of the energy of the sun into plant food through the process of photosynthesis. It is achieved as follows: Leaves absorb carbon dioxide from the air through tiny pores in the leaf surface. Then,

with energy from sunlight combined with chlorophyll—the green pigment in the leaves —water drawn up from the roots is split into hydrogen and oxygen. The absorbed carbon dioxide combines with the hydrogen to make a carbohydrate, or plant food, and the oxygen is returned to the atmosphere.

Carbohydrates are produced during the day and then at night, when photosynthesis ceases, are delivered as food to every part of the plant. Surpluses can be stored as reserves in bulbs or tubers, like potatoes. At night plants release small quantities of carbon dioxide, and for this reason it is better not to have too many plants in the bedroom.

Why plants are so varied

All plants need light to trigger photosynthesis. However, different plants have adapted themselves to degrees between full sun and

deepest shade and the right amount of light will produce a strong, compact form. A plant receiving too little light will stretch in search of it, elongating cells within the plant, and making it long and straggly. In siting plants it's important to find out their requirements for sun or shade.

As with light levels, plants have adapted themselves to temperature. Many plants become dormant in winter, ticking over with minimal expenditure of effort, like a hibernating bear, until spring sets them into growth again. Other plant variations reflect adaptations to different conditions: thick leaves that retain moisture in a drought, flowers that only open in the evening to attract the right type of pollinator, roots that survive waterlogging, tough foliage that will put up with salt-laden winds.

Peat or no Peat, what should I do?

The peat problem
Peat is light and easy to work with, but its extraction from peat bogs has destroyed rare habitats. To avoid further extraction, a number of peat-free composts have appeared on the market, based on coir (coconut fiber), composted bark, or municipal green waste. They may behave differently from peat, but experiment until you find one that works for you.

Competition for water, nutrients, air, and space has made plants adapt their growth rate and habit. Some plants like to be a little squashed but the majority have developed ways to encroach on any space available. Climbers creep and twine to find light, shrubs become larger, pushing out their neighbors to cover more nutrient-supplying ground. In the garden, careful juxtaposition of plant neighbors and well-judged ruthlessness in cutting back may be required, and a delicate plant may need the gardener's help to survive.

We can grow a huge range of non-native plants, from tiny alpines to subtropical palms. Finding out how a plant grows in its native habitat is key to understanding its requirements and tolerations.

The magic of soil

Because soil nourishes plants, a well-textured, healthy soil produces strong plants and, literally, makes your garden grow.

Soil contains thousands of living organisms. These can be as small as microscopic bacteria or as large as earthworms. Although some are pests or cause diseases, the majority are harmless or even beneficial to human health. These include bacteria that counteract allergies and increase the effectiveness of our immune systems. If you have asked your doctor about immunization against tetanus, you have little else to worry about. Gloves will keep your hands cleaner and stop them drying out, but to feel the earth with bare hands is to feel its quality. Learning about your soil will prove invaluable.

Different types of soil

A typical cross-section of
earth begins with the dark
topsoil in which plants put
down their roots. Below this
is the lighter, airless subsoil
in which little lives. Beneath
this is bedrock. Only the
topsoil, which can vary in
depth from less than a trowel's
blade to two feet (60cm), will
nourish the plants, but what
lies below has an influence
on its nature.

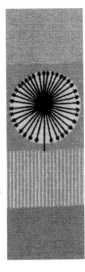

Acidity and alkalinity

The amount of calcium or lime your soil
contains will affect how plants grow. This is
measured on the pH scale, which runs from
1 (peat bog) to 14 (chalk cliff), although most
soils fall within 4.0 to 8.0.

You can easily check the pH of your soil with
one of the widely available soil-testing kits or
electric meters. Take several readings to find
an average, because measurements will vary
around the garden and also according to rain,
temperature, and the season.

To raise pH in an acid soil: Add ground
limestone (calcium carbonate) or dolomitic

SOIL TYPE	DESCRIPTION	ADVANTAGES	DISADVANTAGE
clay	feels sticky and heavy; consists of fine particles that adhere together in a ball when squeezed	can be rich in plant nutrients; retains moisture well	sticky when wet, hard when dry, making it difficult to cultivate; prone to waterlogging; slow to warm in spring
silt	adheres together but with soapy, silky feel, leaves fingers dirty	less rich than clay but good fertility; retains moisture if not compacted	compacts easily; becomes airless; cold and sticky when wet, dusty when dry
sand	large grains feel gritty; crumbles when rolled into a ball	warms up quickly; easy to cultivate; drains easily	nutrients are easily washed out
peat	dark and spongy; doesn't stick together; acid	easy to work; rich in organic matter; retains moisture providing it hasn't dried out	can be very dry in summer and wet in winter; high acidity may be a disadvantage
chalky or calcareous	pale, with lumps of chalk or flint; alkaline	free-draining; good for lime-loving plants.	often very shallow topsoil; nutrients drain away fast; not good for acid-loving plants

acid			neutral		alkaline	
pH 3	**4**	**5**	**6**	**7**	**8**	**9**
toxic to most plants	acid-lovers only	good for most fruit	good for most plants	good for most plants	lime-lovers only	toxic to most plants

limestone (calcium magnesium carbonate), which also adds magnesium. Hydrated lime, sold for mixing with cement, is quicker acting but needs to be replenished annually. Calcified seaweed is also good and adds trace elements. Apply lime several weeks before planting or sowing. Do not apply at the same time as manure because it combines to form ammonia.

To lower soil pH in a very alkaline soil is more difficult because additives quickly leach out of fast-draining soils. Bulky compost or well-rotted manure helps, and if excess lime causes nutrient deficiencies, a raised bed will prevent alkaline solutions penetrating from the surrounding soil.

The acidity or alkalinity of your soil is not about fertility but about the availability of nutrients. In extreme cases it is best to grow plants that are adapted to the conditions, but with the right management, most garden soils can be built into a good loam with balanced pH.

Improving the soil
Whatever your soil type, bulky organic matter is good news: as well as adding nutrients it breaks up heavy clay and helps retain moisture in free-draining soils. It is continually depleted by soil organisms breaking it down and by plants feeding on its goodness, so it must be regularly reapplied.

What plants need
The main nutrients and trace elements a plant needs are dissolved within water drawn up from the soil. Nitrogen for growth in leaves and shoots, phosphorus for roots, and potassium for the development of flowers and fruit are the major nutrients. They are required in relatively large amounts and plants absorb them whether they are from an artificial fertilizer or from an organic one. However, artificial fertilizers can destroy soil bacteria, which is detrimental to the soil.

Trace elements are minerals that are required in very small quantities but an imbalance in any one will affect growth. This is unlikely to occur in soils with plenty of organic matter. Spraying with liquid seaweed and mulching with manure or compost will usually correct any deficiencies.

What's growing next door?

You can tell a lot about soil by what is already growing in your own and in your neighbors' gardens, and in the wild nearby. Rhododendrons and most heathers will only grow in acid soil, while wild clematis (old man's beard) flourishes in an alkaline soil. Talk to neighbors with established gardens about which plants thrive.

How to feed the soil

There are many different sorts of fertilizers, additives, and improvers—choose a type that is best for your conditions. The lime content of mushroom compost, for instance, will increase the alkaline levels of an acid soil. Peat soils are usually rich in organic matter but low in nutrients and will need the addition of fertilizers in granular form. On clay and silt soils, dig in soil improvers in autumn or winter. On quick-draining sand, they are better applied near to the surface in spring.

Many of the soil improvers listed below can be bought in a ready-to-apply state from garden centers, but make use of any other local sources, including your own garden. Most organic matter needs to be allowed to decompose (compost) to stabilize nutrients or reduce toxins.

Animal manures

Animal manures improve soil structure and its water-holding capacity, and are good for hungry feeders in the vegetable garden (potatoes, zucchini [courgettes], pumpkins, tomatoes and brassicas) and as a mulch around roses. However, they must be well-rotted before use. Add to the regular compost pile or, if you have a fresh source delivered, make a special pile. Pack it down so that there are no air pockets, water well, and cover with polythene. It will be ready in twelve months.

Straw-based cattle and horse manures: These derive their goodness from urine, so its best if they haven't been left out in the rain, which washes out the nitrogen and potassium. From an uncovered farm pile, take it from under the surface where it will already have started rotting.

Shavings-based manures: Treat with care. A covered pile takes three or four years to rot down completely. Dug into the earth too soon, the shavings will rob the soil of nitrogen. Grass mowings, nettles, or comfrey (all high in nitrogen) will accelerate their decomposition. If in doubt apply as a surface mulch around shrubs, but not on poor soils.

Poultry and pigeon manure: very high in nitrogen and should not be used neat. Mix with straw and rot as above, or use as a compost activator. Manure from pets like rabbits or hamsters can be treated the same way. Pelleted chicken manure is highly concentrated; use it as a fertilizer rather than a manure, and apply according to instructions.

Organic soil improvers and mulches

type	fertility	application
animal manures	high	Dig in well-rotted manures to improve soil texture anywhere in garden; also use as *mulch* for trees, shrubs or herbaceous perennials. *Alternative sources:* farms, stables (see page 14).
shredded bark	low	As decorative mulch and weed suppressant under shrubs or on paths and borders. *Alternative sources:* municipal recycling or hire a shredder to make your own.
cocoa shells (waste produce from chocolate factories)	high, acidic	Good substitute for peat. Dig in as soil conditioner or use as mulch in most parts of the garden. Good for lowering pH on alkaline soils.
coir (coconut fiber)	low (except in potassium), acidic	As soil conditioner, in potting composts and to lower pH for acid-loving plants. As mulch, apply moist in a thin layer.
garden compost	high	Dig in to improve soil texture and supply nutrients anywhere, including potting soil mixtures. *Alternative source:* make your own (see page 17).
spent mushrooms compost	high, alkaline	Dig in to improve soil structure and counteract acidity or use as general mulch. Allow to decompose under cover for several months before use. Not for acid-loving plants. *Alternative source:* mushroom farms.
worm compost	high	Mix small amounts into top of soil or use as top-dressing for pots, containers, and hanging baskets. Fine texture good for mixing with potting composts.
hay	medium	Effective mulch anywhere except around young plants susceptible to snails/slugs. Breaks down to condition soil. Can provide all nutrients necessary for raspberries and fruit bushes. Store for several months if newly harvested. *Alternative sources:* farms, stables, feed merchants.
straw	low	As hay, except has little nutrient value. Spread under strawberries to keep fruit clean and heap over rhubarb.
evergreen prunings	low	Shred and leave to weather for several months to get rid of toxins. Apply as mulch but avoid using on young plants. *Alternative sources:* landscape gardeners, tree surgeons, municipal recycling.
soft prunings/ hedge clippings	low	Use fresh as a mulch for trees, shrubs and perennials. Add shredded or chopped to compost heap. *Alternative source:* own or neighbors' gardens.
woody prunings	low	As mulch to suppress weeds. Leave in pile to mature as this will kill any diseases, and shred before use (see shredded bark). *Alternative sources:* landscape gardeners, tree surgeons, muncipal recycling, forestry.
sawdust/ wood shavings	low	As mulch on paths and other non-growing areas. Takes several years to rot down (will rob the soil of nitrogen if dug in when fresh). *Alternative sources:* lumber yards (make sure it hasn't been treated), forestry.
seaweed	high, especially potassium and trace elements	Activates compost piles and improves soil structure. Use fresh, composted, dug in, or as a mulch. Also in liquid or meal form from garden centers. *Alternative source:* unpolluted beaches (permit may be needed). Avoid old dry seaweed as this could be salty.

Mulching

Soil improvers can be dug in to the soil, or they can be spread on top as a mulch.
A good blanket of mulch will:

♦ suppress weeds
♦ keep the soil beneath cooler in summer and warmer in winter (so increasing the growing season)
♦ protect the soil from heavy rain
♦ reduce water loss
♦ encourage earthworms and other beneficial soil organisms

As an organic mulch slowly decomposes, it will be drawn down into the earth by worms, thereby improving the quality of the soil. And finally, it's a lot less work to apply a mulch than to do a lot of digging.

Apply a mulch when the soil is warm since it acts as an insulating barrier and will inhibit a cold soil from warming up. Before applying, water the soil well because water will only permeate through it slowly. Keep organic mulches away from the stems of most plants, because they can scorch or rot. The exceptions to this rule are tomatoes and brassicas, which will make new roots into the mulch and grow more vigorously for it.

Mulch does have some disadvantages. Not all mulches are attractive. Rapidly decaying mulches, like compost, grass clippings, and hay, encourage slugs and snails. However, there is also an argument that this moist, rich environment encourages good predators, like ground beetles. Some harbor weed seeds which germinate on the surface, but these

Grass clippings
In large amounts, grass clippings will exclude air and turn into a damp sludge. However, they begin to rot very quickly (you can feel the heat from clippings within half a day) and when they are mixed with other ingredients, they will speed up decomposition.

can be easily pulled out or smothered by a new layer of mulch.

Use the table of soil improvers on page 15 as a guide to which would be the best for your garden's conditions.

Sheet mulches

A site for a new vegetable bed, border or even a lawn can be started without digging, by using a sheet mulch.

Clear the ground of all woody vegetation. Knock over and tread down soft weeds. If high fertility is needed, scatter a high-nitrogen manure. Then, cover the area with a permeable multi-layered barrier mulch to exclude light, and water the whole area to help it to bed down.

As the base layer decomposes, the other layers will be drawn into the soil by worms. Young plants (but not seedlings) can be planted through the layers into the soil in the first year: stab a hole with a screwdriver to get access for your trowel and add a handful of compost before planting.

Making garden compost

Transforming waste materials into nutritious

plant food can be immensely satisfying.

Compost could be made by simply forming a pile and leaving it to rot, but this kind of pile can be difficult to remove, and you may not want to come home to hillocks of half-rotten vegetable matter. A contained pile also works more efficiently.

You can buy special bins or build your own from wooden planks, wire mesh insulated with newspapers or plastic, or even a bottomless garbage can. The larger it is, the better it works. Site it on bare earth or grass, preferably with some shade to make retaining moisture easier. Air is important to the decomposition process, so try to use a base that will provide an updraught: boards over a trench, with gaps for the air to circulate, or perhaps a pallet or upturned plastic crate.

Decomposition with air is called aerobic and is quick, while decomposition without air is called anaerobic and is slow. Most piles start as aerobic and end up as anaerobic. In the truly aerobic pile, the energy from billions of bacteria breaking down the compost's ingredients generates temperatures high enough to destroy weed seeds, pests, and diseases. Compost can be ready in as little as six weeks, but most garden compost is made much more slowly.

Compost ingredients			
quick to rot (hot)	**medium**	**slow to rot (cold)** chop, tear or shred to aid decomposition	**avoid**
salad greens grass clippings soft weeds nettles/comfrey green manures (see page 93) poultry manure (without straw) fresh animal manure (see page 14) seaweed compost activators	vegetable/fruit waste Tea bags/tea leaves coffee grounds animal manures with straw soft hedge prunings ashes	thick vegetable stems straw and hay (wet) old bedding plants autumn leaves (a few) woody prunings (shred) newspaper/cardboard (wet) wool wood shavings (mix in well) nuts and shells eggshells (crush/burn) animal hair (mix in well)	meat or fish fats dog and cat faeces

Balance material that is quick to rot—to start the process—with ingredients that take their time but will give body and texture to the compost.

Either store material and layer the pile at one time or start with a woody layer and continue adding kitchen waste and other ingredients as they become available. Don't press the air out of the pile and incorporate some springy material such as fibrous plant stems. Turning the pile will also aerate it. Cover it so that rain does not wash away the nutrients, and if the compost becomes too dry, water to revive the microorganisms and speed up decomposition. When your bin is full, leave for at least six months, preferably a year, and start another.

You can tell when compost is ready by its dark, friable quality. Compost should not smell (this could could mean it is too wet and still rotting) and none of the original ingredients should be discernible.

Making leafmold

Although the nutrient value is negligible, leafmold is a good soil conditioner. It takes longer to rot down than compost and, instead of bacteria, fungi are the primary decomposers.

Use fallen leaves from deciduous trees and shrubs, but don't collect those from busy roadsides, which may be polluted. Build a simple container with netting and posts or store collected leaves in plastic bags—pierce the bags with a few holes and tie the tops loosely. One-year-old leafmold makes a good mulch. However, after two years it will be much finer and can be sieved and added to potting compost.

Home-made liquid nettle fertilizer

This is a good general fertilizer, low on phosphate but high in magnesium, sulphur, and iron. Young nettles cut in spring are the most nutritious. Steep 2lb (1kg) of leaves in a bucket with about 2 gallons (10 liters) of water and cover. (The smell from this concoction is strong.) Use after two weeks, diluted 1:10 with water.

To dig or not to dig, that is the question.

Dig or no dig?

Digging aerates the soil, allows you to incorporate organic matter, and gets rid of perennial weeds. However, it also disturbs bacterial activity and brings more weed seeds to the surface. Whether you choose to dig or not will depend on your soil and what time, strength, and aims you have.

Usually, soil only needs to be dug to one spade's depth (single digging). However, double digging, the double depth of a spade, may be needed if soil is heavily compacted (perhaps from heavy building machinery or prolonged waterlogging). Double digging should only need to be done once.

Digging tips

Walking on heavy soil when it is wet will compact it—put down boards to stand on.

Use a spade that is the right size for you and lift spadefuls that are not too heavy or you will not last—digging is a slow, methodical occupation.

Keep the spade close to you so that you are not reaching forward.

If possible, wait until conditions are right: working waterlogged or sun-baked earth is much harder.

HOW TO DIG
Single digging a large area

To dig a large area like a vegetable garden, divide the plot in two.

◆ Dig a trench, about 12in wide and the depth of one spade blade deep, from the top left hand side of the plot to the center line. Put the earth into a wheelbarrow.

◆ Empty the earth from it in a heap beside the opposite half of the plot and at the same end you have started working from. This will be used to fill in the last trench when you get there.

◆ Fill the first trench with approximately 3in of well-rotted manure or garden compost, spreading it out evenly.

◆ Working backward, dig the second trench on the half plot in front of the first. Throw the earth from the second trench into the first trench, turning the earth over so that what was at the bottom is now at the top. At the same time, take out rooting weeds like docks and thistles. The smaller weeds will be buried.

◆ Continue like this to the end of the first half plot and then work back along the second half, until you are back beside where you made the first trench. When you have dug this out, filled it with compost or manure, refill it with the soil from the first trench.

Coping with shallow topsoil

Deep digging may not be possible in very shallow soil. In this case, dig down as far as possible, breaking up a little of the inert subsoil and mixing it with fertile compost. This and repeated applications of thick mulch (see pages 15–16) will, over time, increase the depth of topsoil.

Double-digging

To double-dig a large area, start as for single digging, by dividing the plot down the center.

◆ Mark with a line a 2 feet (60cm) wide strip across the top of the first half of the plot to be dug. Take out the earth up to the depth of one spade and put it into a wheelbarrow or heap by the last trench

◆ Using a fork, break up the earth a further spade's depth (or whatever is possible) down in the bottom of the trench.

◆ As with single digging, fill a wheelbarrow with compost or well-rotted manure and fill the trench, spreading it evenly, and mixing it into the top 4–6 inches (10–15cm).

◆ Mark out the next 2 foot (60cm) wide trench, dig it, turning the earth over and dropping it into the first trench. Fork the surface loose, add the manure, and mark out the next trench.

◆ Continue until the last trench and fill this with soil from the first trench.

No dig

In no-dig gardening, the soil is never disturbed. Fertility and soil structure are improved by applying mulches and nutrients to the surface, leaving worms and soil organisms to break it down to make a rich, friable topsoil. A sheet mulch (see page 16) keeps weed seeds from germinating.

No-dig gardening:

◆ protects the soil structure, making it more able to retain moisture and release nutrients, and avoids the effort of digging.

Turning the soil over

This is easier than single or double digging and is good for heavy soils or to generally aerate, weed, and incorporate compost. It's a good way to work across a border and around plants that are already there, making sure you give them a wide margin so as to not damage their roots.

◆ With a spade (or a fork if the soil is very heavy), start in the corner of one end of the area you are working on.

◆ With your foot on the spade, put it into the ground at a slight angle, about 60 degrees. Press the handle of the spade down so that earth is lifted at the blade end. Lift this and turn it over.

◆ Break the clod up with the blade of the spade and take any weeds out by loosening them with your hand. Heavy-rooted weeds like docks, and creeping ones like bindweed and quack grass, should be burnt or put in the garbage and not on the compost pile.

◆ Continue methodically, as if you were digging trenches. Fork compost or well-rotted manure into the first turned over earth. Turn over the next "trench" area and work backward so you don't step on the earth you have worked and manured.

◆ means fewer weed seeds are brought to the surface, but can take longer to improve poor soil.

◆ does not expose pests within the soil to frost or predators (although there is some argument about this).

◆ mulches can be unsightly, but no more than in a dug garden.

Ways with water

Like us, plants need water to live. A shortage causes nutrient deficiencies in the soil and weakens plants, making them more susceptible to pests and disease. Irregular watering puts plants under stress. Not knowing when they may next receive a dousing, they take drastic action: leafy food plants bolt (i.e. race to produce flower and seed in an effort to reproduce themselves before they meet their end), annuals flower quickly and die, and trees and shrubs shed their leaves prematurely. On the other hand, too much water can adversely affect all but water and bog plants.

When to water?

Apart from obvious clues such as rainfall and temperature, there are more elusive factors that will tell you when a plant needs water. Watching your plants will train a kind of sixth sense, warning you before they reach the drooping stage. Leaves and flowers may lack vigor or luster, stems take on a transparent look, and the lawn loses its springiness. Don't just look at the soil's surface; put a finger into the earth to feel it. Some soils, especially in containers, can be wet on the surface but still dry underneath.

Avoid watering in the heat of the day when evaporation is at its greatest. Water early in the morning or even better, at the end of the day. Be careful not to water plants in full sunshine as droplets on the leaves act like a magnifying glass and can scorch them.

Always water immediately after planting. This makes sure that air pockets are sealed temporarily so that the root hairs don't dry out. Give a good soaking and then leave until the plant really needs water. This ensures that it will endeavor to find its own water.

Keep a special eye on containers. They dry out more quickly than soil in the open garden, and a vigorously growing hanging basket may need watering twice a day in hot, dry weather.

Plants have different water requirements at different stages of growth. Seedlings may need daily or even twice-daily watering, but as they grow, their root systems should search deeper into the ground. Newly planted trees and shrubs will need watering in dry conditions for one or two years until they become established. Vegetables will welcome extra water as they plump up.

Watering tips

• Consider which plants need watering, rather than just watering everything robotically.
• Give plants a thorough soaking occasionally rather than small amounts frequently.
• Water slowly to give time for the water to sink into the ground.
• Aim at the roots rather than soaking the leaves and stems.
• A short length of piping half-buried beside a plant will ensure the water reaches the roots.
• Plants at the foot of a wall can dry out even in wet weather—the wall creates a "rain shadow" that prevents rain penetrating close to its base.
• Hand-watering is time-consuming, but it lets you see how individual plants are thriving.

Unwanted carpet

To provide a moisture-retaining skirt for a new plant, cut a square or circle of old carpet slightly larger than the root system. Slit it to the center and slip it around the plant's stem to lie on the soil. Disguise with a thin covering of shredded bark or soil.

Watering systems

All sorts of irrigation systems are available. Sprinklers deliver a thorough soaking gently, but it can be tricky to position them correctly. More effective is a soaker-hose laid on the soil around plants that dampens the ground slowly as water permeates the porous hose wall. The most sophisticated systems can be finely tuned to suit your requirements, with timers, and moisture and temperature sensors.

Watering cans and roses

Apply water with a can that has different gauges of roses to govern the size of spray: seedlings require very fine spray; older plants can take bigger droplets. When watering seedling flats or pots, set them in a tray of water to soak until the top of the soil is moist. Watering cans with long necks can reach into containers, along window boxes, and to the back of borders. Hand watering allows you to ensure that water gets to the roots of each plant.

A tip for plump beans

Several layers of newspaper laid in the bottom of the trench before planting beans will help conserve moisture and will have rotted by the end of the season.

Conserving water

With ever-increasing demands on our water supply, we should take steps to reduce what we use. Conserving moisture efficiently also makes watering less of a chore. The following help:

♦ collecting rainwater, which is also better for some plants, such as acid-lovers in containers.

♦ improving soil structure (see pages 14–16); a fibrous, spongy soil retains water better.

♦ mulching (see pages 15–16).

♦ covering bare soil with shallow-rooting groundcover plants to minimize evaporation.

Poor drainage

In some soils the problem is too much water. If water sits on the surface and cannot filter through, double digging and the incorporation organic matter should restore soil structure.

Plants are a solution for poor drainage. Their roots penetrate the soil, aerating it and making drainage channels. In a soggy vegetable patch, grow fruit bushes with basket-making willow (*Salix viminalis*).

Where heavy clay soil over a clay subsoil varies between a bog in winter and cement in summer, or if the water table is close to the surface, you may need to install land drains. These can empty into a storm drain (may require permission), but not into the main sewage system. Where there is no suitable drain you will need to dig a soakaway.

Soakaway system

Dig a trench about at least 24 inches (60cm) deep. Lay a perforated pipe in it, sloping toward a soakaway—a hole in the ground

Help! My garden is turning into a bog!

Plants to combat waterlogging:
willows (*Salix* spp.)
poplars (*Populus* spp.)
alders (*Alnus* spp.)

about 3 feet (90cm) square and 6 feet (180cm) or more deep filled with rubble or gravel to 1 foot (30cm) below the surface. Spread gravel along the trench to a depth of 1 foot (30cm). Cover the gravel with plastic so soil does not fall between the stones. Fill to the surface with soil.

Mulching

Soil loses moisture through surface evaporation as well as via plants, but mulch protects it from the sun and drying winds. Be generous with the mulch, but don't smother small plants—a thickness of 4 inches (10cm) keeps soil moist and suppresses weeds. Coir only needs a thin layer but moisten it beforehand. Bark chips look smart and retain moisture beneath, but may be less permeable from above.

Only organic mulches feed and improve the structure of the soil, but for moisture conservation consider two inorganic mulches:

black polyethylene: also suppresses weeds. Not pretty, but good in a vegetable patch. Plant through holes cut in the plastic. Lift after a few months to let air and water into the ground. Permeable woven fabric mulches are best, and readily available.

gravel: keeps the earth cool and helps drainage around plants that like dry conditions, such as alpines and succulents.

Ways with weeds

Weeds are wild plants—often beautiful in the countryside, but not always in the garden—which compete for nutrients, water, and space.

Not all weeds are bad, which is why a weed can be defined as a plant in the wrong place. There are pretty ones like golden rod, poppies and wild pansies, and even a nettle patch will attract butterflies. Lambs quarters, chickweed, shepherd's purse, and purslane can be added to salads. Young nettle leaves taste a bit like spinach when used in soup or pasta. With some, like tansy, we may welcome the flowers but not their prolific habit.

Bad companions

Buckwheat and winter rye, grown and dug in as a green manure, release chemicals that inhibit the germination of seeds for several weeks. Young plants can be planted on the plot and benefit from a weed-free start.

Identifying the different weeds in your garden is the first step to knowing whether you want to get rid of them or not, and understanding the way a weed propagates itself gives clues to how to prevent it spreading.

Annual weeds

These weeds grow, flower, scatter their seed, and die in the same year. Catch them before they seed. Examples: shepherd's purse (*Capsella bursa-pastoris*), purslane (*Portulaca olcraooa*), chickweed (*Stellaria media*), wild mustard (*Brassica kaber*), and ragweed (*Ambrosia artemisii folia*).

Biennial weeds

These also reproduce from seed but take two years to complete their life cycle. They have a deep taproot (see below) and overwinter as a rosette of leaves. Again, the trick is to stop the seed from spreading.

Burdock (*Arctium* spp.), **common mullein** (*Verbscum thapsus*), **Queen Anne's lace** (*Daucus carota*), **white cockle** (*Silene alba*), and **teasel** (*Dipsacus fullonum*).

Perennial weeds

These are the weeds that persist and establish themselves. They spread not only by seed, but from pieces, sometimes minute fragments, of root or stem or from bulbils or runners. It is safer not to put these on the compost pile.

Those in bold below are particularly unwelcome squatters and can test the patience of the most tolerant gardener. You may never eradicate them completely, but they need to be severely controlled or they will swamp all else. In an infested area that you can leave fallow for several seasons, a good method is to cover the whole area with a permeable, light-excluding membrane for two years or more. An alternative for really persistent weeds like horsetail or Canada thistle might be to sow grass seed and mow for several seasons.

Tap roots

Long and tenacious, these can be single or branched.

Dandelion (*Taraxacum* spp.), **dock** (*Rumex* spp.), **comfrey** (*Symphytum officinalis*), **cow parsley** (*Anthriscus sylvestris*)

You can patiently tease the roots out whole with the aid of a fork, but digging or rotovating will spread them. Continually hoeing off the leaves will weaken them, especially just after flowering when the root will be weakened by the energy put into producing flowers. Docks regenerate from any part of the top 6 inches (15cm) and also seed prolifically, so cut off the flower spikes to limit their spread.

Shallow spreading roots or rhizomes

nettles (*Urtica dioica*), **quack grass** (*Agropyron repens*), **prostrate pigweed** (*Amaranthus blitoides*), **knotweed** (*Polygonum aviculare*).

The shallow roots can be pulled or forked and teased out by hand fairly easily even if matted, but any bits left behind will send up new shoots. Rototilling several times will bring the roots up to the surface. Cutting them before they set seed will weaken them. A light-excluding mulch for one season will also get rid of them. If quack grass is enmeshed with ornamentals, dig up infested plants, wash roots, pot up and observe for a season to ensure that none of this weed survives.

Deep spreading storage roots

Kudzu (*Pueraria lobata*), **poison ivy** (*Rhus radicus*), **field bindweed** (*Convolvulus arvensis*), **horsetail** (*Equisetum spp.*), **creeping thistle** (*Cirsium arvense*).

These send up shoots if the top is cut and are difficult to control. Horsetail's black creeping underground stems can penetrate 6 feet (2m) or more. Continual hoeing and forking will weaken them, as will a light-excluding mulch for two years or planting grass and mowing for two seasons.

Runners

Creeping buttercup (*Ranunculus repens*), **cinquefoil** (*Potentilla reptans*), **ground ivy** (*Glechoma hederacea*), **silverweed** (*Potentilla anserina*), **selfheal** (*Prunella vulgaris*).

Stems creep over the ground and produce plantlets that detach and grow separately, in turn producing more runners. Fork them up or, on a large scale, rototill several times or apply a light-excluding mulch for one year.

Weeding can be such hard work –but it's worth it!

Weed brew

Put weeds in a barrel or bucket and cover with water. Stir occasionally and when they have completely decomposed, spray where weeds are troublesome. Old country lore says you should spray three times when the moon is in Cancer and repeat the following month and the next if necessary. The brew is said to be especially effective against creeping and climbing weeds.

Corms or bulbils

Lesser celandine (*Ranunculus ficaria*), **wild onion** (*Allium canadense*).

Hoeing or digging will spread these weeds. If taking up individual plants, take up the soil around them too. Bulbils survive for a long time underground, so a light-excluding mulch will need to be in place for two years.

Low-growing, tight rosettes of leaves

Sheep sorrel (*Rumex aectosella*), **plantain** (*Plantago spp.*), **hawkweed** (*Hieracium spp.*), **yarrow** (*Achillea millefolium*).

These are mainly a nuisance in lawns because the rosettes spread outward forming a mat, and the seed also spreads to new sites. Hoeing or forking will remove them. If they have covered a large area, rototill or cover with a light-excluding mulch for one year.

Power weeding

A hand fork is invaluable for working among plants and being selective in what you remove, and a hoe makes quick work of cutting off weed seedlings at soil level, but there are also some useful power tools:

Flame weeder: Wilts and kills with a short blast of heat from a flame. Best for paths, drives or patios.

String trimmer: Cuts with either a fast-rotating nylon line or, for heavier jobs like clearing brambles, a metal disc.

Rototiller: Useful for clearing ground and breaking up the earth. However, it will also chop up perennial weeds with creeping stems or taproots, potentially aggravating the

problem. Remove these weeds beforehand or rotovate several times as new weeds grow.

Chemical weedkillers

Chemicals are modern magic, but most are not accepted by organic gardeners because of the danger to the many insects and natural life for which weeds provide shelter and food. Indiscriminate elimination of weeds destroys habitats, but here are some guidelines for discriminate use:

♦ Always follow the manufacturer's instructions and store in the original containers, with labels and explanations, in a cool place out of reach of children or animals.

♦ When applying with a watering can, ensure an even covering.

♦ Wear rubber gloves and old clothes.

♦ Avoid contact with skin and eyes and do not inhale dust, smoke, or spray.

♦ Do not eat, smoke, or drink when applying chemicals.

♦ Spray when weather is dry and windless to prevent the chemicals from drifting.

♦ Spray in the evening when pollinating insects are less active.

♦ Use a shield, such as a sheet of cardboard, to prevent spray from going on garden plants.

♦ Spray weeds when they are actively growing (in warmer months).

♦ Rinse all equipment thoroughly before and after use, and do not use the same equipment for pesticides.

♦ Never flush excess chemicals into the sewage system. Apply excess to gravel paths or waste ground.

The magic of seeds

The aim of a plant is to flower and set seed so that it can reproduce itself. To do this, pollen from the male stamens is transferred to the female pistils either within the same flower or a different one. Whether pollen is carried on the wind, the legs of insects, or the beaks of birds, the result is a seed.

Buying seed

It is tempting to get carried away by the colorful packets of seed in stores and mail order catalog. Try to be realistic about how many seedlings you can actually raise successfully.

A seed packet carries quite a lot of information. As well as cultivation notes, it will give the approximate number of seeds it contains, an expected germination time and a sow-by date. Seeds may be sown after this date, but the germination rate will probably be lower. Seed viability varies—primroses and meconopsis are best sown as fresh as possible, but some seeds last for many years. Experience will tell you what proportion of seeds you can expect to make it through to full-sized plants. If sowing older seed, you will need to sow proportionately more.

Pelleted seeds are more expensive, but can prove more economical. Each seed is encased in a degradable coating, which makes it easier to handle and space, so there is less need for thinning later.

Different characteristics, such as new colors, shapes, or heights, occur through cross-fertilization. This happens accidentally in nature, but is also carried out by plant breeders, and a majority of the plants in our gardens are hybrids. Some plants reliably produce offspring just like themselves, generation after generation, but many open-pollinated, or non-hybrid, seeds include variable characteristics from both parents. The more expensive F1 hybrids, however, are guaranteed to germinate (but seed you collect from them and sow yourself won't).

Collecting seed

It's a wonderful feeling to harvest seed, whether from your own garden or that of a neighbor or friend, and cleaning and sorting seed is therapeutic on a winter's evening.

Harvest only from healthy plants. Store the seedpods in envelopes or paper bags to dry or hang whole stems upside down with their heads encased in a cone of newspaper so the seeds can drop into the newspaper as they dry. Remember to label collected seed with the month, year, and name of the plant.

Once the seed cases are dry, they can be crumbled in the hand or sieved to release the seed. Poppy seed cases are like little vases with aerated lids; just tap them and the seed will pour out. Berries and fruit will need to be soaked before mashing to release the seed from the pulp.

Store dry, cleaned seed in airtight containers in a cold, dry place. Cold temperatures, even below freezing, are better than warmth or moisture.

Imagine the process in the wild

Berries and seeds are eaten by birds or animals, stomach acid breaks down hard outer casings, and the seed is then excreted with its own manure patch to feed on once it has lain dormant through the winter. We can simulate this process by scratching any tough coating and storing the seed for about three months in the fridge (the manure can come later!).

Sowing in pots, containers, and cell packs

A seed's first requirements are air, warmth and moisture. Nutrition comes later —seedlings started on a rich diet grow too quickly and become sappy and susceptible to disease. You can sow directly into the open ground (see page 42) or, for more control over early growing conditions, start off your seeds in containers.

Small pots (3 inches or 7.5cm) or specially-designed cell packs are useful, but so are recycled food containers or even cardboard egg boxes. Plastic is easy to keep clean, while biodegradable containers, such as fiber or compressed peat pots, have the benefit of rotting without your having to disturb the young plants. All containers will need drainage holes to prevent waterlogging and to allow water to be taken up from below.

Most seedlings are happy in 1inch (2–3cm) of compost, but this can dry out very quickly, so a depth of 2 inches (5cm) is safer. Choose an all-purpose compost which states it is suitable for seed (meaning it has few or no nutrients). It should be even in texture and retain water well.

A good "recipe" for seeds:
3 parts finely sieved leafmold (or wood-land topsoil well mulched by leaves or pine needles)
1 part fine sand
For cuttings: add perlite instead of sand to increase drainage.

Potting compost:
3 parts leafmold
1 part garden compost, well sieved
1 part coarse sand or perlite

Make your own compost
Composts consist of:
a base: topsoil or old potting compost (sterilized)
for bulk: two-year-old leafmold, composted bark, coir, or composted municipal green waste
for drainage: sand (free of salt or other contaminants), perlite, or vermiculite (light volcanic stones)
fertilizer: garden or worm compost or animal manure (all well-rotted)
To kill off weed seeds and any harmful organisms, sterilize by placing in a shallow tray. Cover with foil and bake in the oven at 180°F (80°C) for 30 mins.

Sowing

Fill each container with seed compost and firm down slightly. Either scatter small seeds thinly across the surface or draw thin lines in the compost and drizzle seed thinly into them. Press larger or pelleted seeds gently into the compost about ½ inch (1cm) apart. Cover with a light sprinkling of compost (or perlite if the packet instructions say the seeds need a lot of light to germinate) and gently tap the sides of the containers to help the soil to settle.

Next, soak the containers in a tray or sink of water. Alternatively, use a watering can with a very fine rose, swung so that only the fine, even center of the arc of water falls on the soil. Allow to drain.

Protecting

Cover the containers with clear polyethylene or place inside a transparent plastic bag to encourage warmth and maintain moisture. Allow room for the seeds to germinate.

Place the containers in an evenly warm place. A window sill has the best light levels, but temperatures fluctuate a lot, so move the containers at night or if the sun shines directly on them. A warm cupboard is ideal for tender and half-hardy seeds but move them into the light as soon as they germinate.

Although the seeds are under plastic, avoid drafts. You can insulate and increase the light on a window sill by lining the surface and the first 6 inches (15cm) of glass with aluminium foil that will reflect light back onto the germinating seedlings.

Watering and feeding

Check daily that the compost inside the containers is still moist. Should it dry out despite the polyethylene covering, water from below again. Once shoots appear take the covers off to let the air circulate. Shade the seedlings from hot sun, if necessary, and use a fine water spray to maintain moisture levels.

As seedlings grow they need food. A weak solution of liquid seaweed fertilizer will help growth, but their root systems will soon fill the pot or tray. When the seedlings are large enough to handle and before they become too crowded, they should be pricked out.

Pricking out, potting on

Prepare larger containers in the same way you prepared the seed containers. Use a multi-purpose compost or one with slightly more nutrients. Water the seedlings and the new soil mix they are being transplanted into.

Seedlings will generally have two to four small leaves. The lowest pair, the seed leaves, will wither away in time, so hold seedlings by these, rather than the stem and roots. Ease the seedling out with a blunt knife. Make a hole with a pencil or small dibble (dibber) in the new container and insert the seedling so that the lowest leaves are just above the surface. Firm the soil gently. Space seedlings about 1½ inches (4cm) apart. Water again from below, and keep out of direct sunlight.

This first stage is called "pricking out". As the plants get larger, they may need transplanting again ("potting on") before being planted in their final homes.

Multi-seeding
This intensive but effective method of sowing seeds minimizes root disturbance; even root vegetables sort themselves out and thrive. Sow small individual pots or cells with a pinch of seed in the center. This will give you two or three times as many plants as you want. Before the seedlings get overcrowded, cut off all but two to five of the strongest plants. Grow on as usual until the roots fill the pot and then plant the whole potful as a clump without splitting it up. Space the clumps slightly wider apart than normal.

Hardening off and planting out

Some plants will tolerate colder conditions than others, but all young plants grown under cover need to be hardened off or acclimatized to the outside world. Set them outside during the day to allow the wind to strengthen their stems, and bring them back in at night. Graduate them to a coldframe or begin to leave them outside at night under a floating row cover (horticultural fleece) or polyethylene. After they have spent about a week or so outside, you can plant them out.

This transition is a shock to a plant, so make it as stress-free as possible. Ensure the pot's soil is moist. Disturb the roots as little as possible and water immediately so that the soil filters down to fill spaces around the roots. Mulch around plants that are large enough not to be suffocated. In hot weather shade the plants for a few days. (A newspaper folded into a triangle or an envelope with one side slit open will make a temporary shade.)

Some plants with large soft leaves, like spinach or cabbage, benefit from having their leaves trimmed back to 2 inches (5cm) or so after planting out to minimize any water loss from them.

I haven't got a coldframe

If you do not have a coldframe, construct a temporary one from a few bricks with a piece of glass or old window frame over the top.

Greenhouses and coldframes

A greenhouse is a great asset, but temperatures will vary more than indoors and it is easier to forget about seedlings if they are out of sight. Do not sow too early —wait until spring is well established and the better light levels and warmer days will promote faster, stronger growth. Use bubble wrap to insulate an unheated greenhouse or to make an inner tent over your seedlings. Begin the hardening off process by increasing the ventilation.

A coldframe is useful for overwintering seeds that need a period of cold or young hardy perennials and vegetables not planted out in the fall. It also makes a useful "halfway house" for hardening off young plants, and tender perennials, tomatoes, peppers and eggplants (aubergines) can all use its protection until the danger of frost has passed.

Sowing outdoors

Wait until the soil is neither too wet nor too cold. Sandy soils warm faster than clay ones. Soil can be warmed in early spring by covering it with plastic or floating row cover (fleece) for a couple of weeks. Mulching with aged animal manure will also warm the soil.

Preparing a seedbed

Choose an open but sheltered position. A temporary surround of 6 inch (15cm) planks will delineate the seedbed, provide a windbreak at ground level, and act as a support for protective netting or row cover (fleece). Seeds do not need many nutrients, so only add low- or no-nutrient soil conditioners (see page 15).

Prepare the soil until it is almost like breadcrumbs. Larger seeds, like beans, sunflowers, or marigolds, will survive rougher ground but lettuces and many annuals need a fine texture. After raking, leave for two weeks to settle, or firm the ground either by walking with little steps across it, or using a plank to walk on and spread your weight more evenly. (For a small area a flat piece of wood pressed down with your hands will be sufficient.) Just before sowing, rake the surface again lightly.

The "stale seedbed" method

If you know there are weed seeds in the soil, rake to a fine tilth then leave for two weeks. Hoe the weeds that appear and sow your seed without further raking. The seeds will grow faster than the next flush of weed seeds, giving them a head start.

Drills, hills (stations), and broadcasting

For sowing directly into a flower bed, see page 42.

Drills: The benefit of sowing in straight rows, or drills, is that the start and finish of a row is marked and weeding can be done either side without disturbing the new seedlings. Use a length of string stretched between two sticks to mark a straight line.

If sowing in dry conditions, water the base of the drill with a trickle of water. If it is very wet, line the drill with seed compost, multi-purpose compost, or vermiculite. This is good for heavy clay soils, which will also benefit from more compost or conditioner being sprinkled lightly over the covered drill.

Take a laid back approach

The suggested sowing time is usually far too early. Seedlings will be weak or suffer from damping off, a fungus disease. Wait three or four weeks, until the days are longer and warmer, and the stronger seedlings will soon catch up lost time.

Hill (station) sowing: This is useful for large or pelleted seeds. Sow two or three seeds together at intervals or hills along the drill, and thin by reducing to the strongest seedling. Hill sowing allows other, faster-growing crops to be sown in between.

Broadcasting: Scattering seed across prepared ground is the oldest form of sowing. It is good for naturalistic and mixed-seed planting, and for crops that don't need thinning. The seed is not going to germinate in easy-to-distinguish rows, so prepare the area by the "stale seedbed" method (see box). Rake gently in different directions to cover the seed, or sieve fine soil over it. There is a risk of the seed drying out because it is near the surface; a covering of clear polyethylene or a row cover (fleece) until germination will help, and gentle watering may be needed in hot weather.

Thinning

With the right conditions, seedlings grow quickly and soon become overcrowded, so the weaker seedlings need to be taken out. To minimize root disturbance, don't pull out the thinnings, simply cut them off at soil level. Remove them to the compost pile because the smell may attract pests.

Protecting young plants

Transparent plastic bottles make excellent mini-cloches over individual plants. Cut off the top and the young plant will be provided with a protecting plastic collar.

Mulching will suppress weed competition and provide nourishment. Keep mulch away from stem and leaves to prevent scorching. Provide early support for plants that will need it; either push twigs into the ground or make a "cage" of stakes (canes) and string. Protect young plants from animals with a chicken wire fence.

chapter 2 *The Plants*

Plants are what a garden is all about. The magic is in the infinite combinations of colors and shapes, the way the passing seasons give rise to different moods, and seeing plants you have nurtured mature and flourish.

Creative designs and color harmonies are found in other books; this chapter aims to help you better understand the plants themselves, which are the building blocks of every garden design. Trees and shrubs are long-term fixtures; invest time and thought in them, but be frivolous and experimental with short-term residents like annuals. Plants in a garden become mutually supportive, both aesthetically and culturally: tall plants give shelter to shorter ones; colorful climbers or naturalized bulbs revive interest in out-of-season shrubs; flowers attract beneficial insects; a hedge is not just a boundary but a living habitat for wildlife.

While improving the soil, providing water and shelter when it is needed, and mastering the elements of pruning will reward you with the best display, gardening is made very much easier if you also choose plants whose requirements fall within the conditions and level of care you can provide.

The Magic of a Night Garden

A garden is a very different place at night, especially under the enchantment of a full moon. A private, enclosed moon garden that only unveils its magic at night might be scented by exotic hanging trumpets of brugmansia *(Datura spp.)*, sweet nicotiana, summer jasmine, and heady gardenia. Choose pale flowers that will stay open and glow in the moonlight, such as camellias and white lilies, and provide a comfortable seat from which to enjoy the tranquillity.

Annuals and biennials

Annuals set seed, flower, and die in the same year, while biennials grow leaves in the first year and then flower, set seed, and die in the second.

Annuals include the giant sunflowers, fragrant sweet peas, and marigolds. They provide color all summer long and, although they need to be replaced each year, are quite easy to grow. Nasturtiums don't mind if the ground is poor and stony and a froth of blue nigella will sow itself again for you next year.

Dedicate a bed to annuals, fill containers with them, or use them to fill space while other plants establish themselves. Many will attract pollinating insects as well as hoverflies for controlling aphids.

Annuals are categorized as hardy or half-hardy. Hardy annuals will withstand cold spring weather and can be sown outside where they are to flower. They can also be started inside or under glass, which produces larger plants better able to withstand pests and outgrow weed competition.

Sowing direct

Prepare the sowing area (see pages 21–22) and outline irregular, naturalistic patches with something that is a different color from the soil, such as sand or ashes. Draw shallow drills 6 inches (15cm) apart across each patch and sow the seed thinly. Cover with soil and water with a fine spray. When the seedlings are large enough to handle, thin them to 6–10 inches (15–25cm) apart, according to cultivar.

Sowing in lines makes it easier to spot the weeds, but you can also broadcast the seed. After scattering, rake carefully so that the seed is covered but spread evenly, or sprinkle fine soil or multi-purpose compost over the top.

Alternatives to sowing

You can also buy annuals and biennials as young plants in trays, cell packs, or plugs (which is how they are supplied by mail order). Starting off with well-rooted plants makes it easy to set them out where you want them to flower but follow the planting advice for half-hardy annuals.

Care

Too rich a soil will encourage leaf growth rather than flowers, but if growth is poor or the lower leaves start to yellow, liquid feeding may be necessary. Provide early support—a wigwam of canes, shrubby twigs, trellis or fencing—for climbing annuals like sweet peas or morning glory (*Ipomoea*). If slugs and snails are a nuisance, set traps and diversions (see page 139).

Hardy annuals

Here's a tiny selection, just to give an idea of the variety available. All of these plants are easy to grow and, given a good start and somewhere reasonably sunny for at least part of the day, should bloom all summer. Those marked * self-seed readily.

California poppy (*Eschscholzia californica*). Glowing yellow, crimson, orange or pink. Height: 12–16 inches (30–40cm). Delicate blue-gray leaves contrast with large satiny petals. Needs full sun; best on poor, light and rather dry soil. Attracts beneficial insects.

Candytuft (*Iberis umbellata*). White, lavender, crimson. Height: 12 inches (30cm). Small rounded flowerheads above thin, dark green leaves. Can also sow in fall for earlier flowering. Good for butterflies.

Batchelor's button (Cornflower) (*Centaurea cyanus*). Sky blue. Height: 12–30 inches (30–75cm). Plant in drifts or wild meadows. Attracts beneficial insects. Good cut flower.

Godetia (*Clarkia amoena* or *Godetia grandiflora*). Red, pink, white. Height: 20 inches (50cm). Bushy plants with vivid, funnel-shaped flowers.

Larkspur (*Consolida ajacis* or *Delphinium ajacis*). Blue, red, violet, white. Height: 10 inches–3 feet (25cm–1m). Lovely, delicate version of its delphinium relation. Can also be sown in fall, for earlier flowers. Stake tall cultivars. Attracts bees.

Love-in-a-mist (*Nigella damascena*).* Blue, also mixed pink, white, and blue varieties. Height: 18 inches (45cm). Thin, delicate plants that need to be in drifts. Feathery foliage. Starry flowers and large, decorative seedpods. Attracts beneficial insects.

Nasturtium (*Tropaeolum majus*). Brilliant yellow, orange, red. Spread: 6 inches–6 feet (15cm–2m). Large, funnel-shaped flowers and fresh, distinctive round foliage. Dwarf and bushy varieties make good groundcover, while climbers will cover fences and trail from baskets. Flowers best in poor, dry, soil (but water until established). All parts edible.

Night-scented stock (*Matthiola bicornis*). Pinks, mauves. Height: 14 inches (35cm). Unremarkable little plants that release the most wonderful fragrance in the evening. Plant in beds or pots under windows or on the patio. Repeat small sowings for a succession of flowers.

Poached egg plant (*Limnanthes douglasii*). White with lemon centres. Spread: 6 inches (15cm). Dark green leaves form a dense carpet and offset the appropriately named flowers. Likes coolness and moisture for roots with head in sun. Good for edging beds. Fragrant flowers attract bees.

Pot marigold (*Calendula officinalis*).* Yellow, cream, apricot, orange. Height: 1–2 feet (30–60cm). Daisy-like flower heads, single or double, that continue almost until winter. Soft, fresh green leaves. Edible petals.

Scabiosa (*Scabiosa atropurpurea*). White, pink, lavender, crimson. Height: 3 feet (90cm). Fragrant pin-cushion flowers on tall, willowy stems. Sow in fall in pots and plant out in spring. Good cut and dried flower.

Sweet alyssum (*Lobularia maritima*). White. Spread: 6–8 inches (15–20cm). Forms neat white hummocks. Happy on hot, dry, alkaline soils. Good for crevices and between paving.

Half-hardy annuals

Half-hardy annuals mostly germinate at around 65°F (18°C). Sow inside or in a heated greenhouse in early spring. Gradually harden off, and plant out when all danger of frost has passed. This allows plants a longer growing season than if they were sown directly into their flowering positions at the end of spring.

When planting out, it is very important to disturb the root system as little as possible. Water well, and remove gently from the pot or from the cell pack. Plant into moist soil, give a good watering, and keep an eye on the young plants until it is apparent that they have established themselves.

Carnation/pink (*Dianthus caryophyllus, D. chinensis*). Delicate pink, rose, white, bi-colors. Height: 6–18 inches (15–45cm). Neat little annual versions of perennial cousins, with sweetly-scented, fringed flowers offset well by gray leaves. Do well on alkaline soil.

Coleus (*Solenostemon scutellarioides*). Red, green, crimson, yellow (foliage). Height: 1½–2 feet (45–60cm). Develops fast into a round, shrubby plant with exotically-marked, multi-colored leaves. Technically a tender shrub, so can be kept from one year to the next given sufficient warmth and light.

Cosmos (*Cosmos bipinnatus*). White, pink, crimson. Height: 2–5 feet (60–1.5cm). Broad-petaled daisies dance above feathery foliage. At the back of a border other plants can support it; otherwise it may need staking. Thrives in poor, sandy soil. Good for butterflies. Deadhead to prolong season but leave some seedheads which may self-sow.

French and African marigolds (*Tagetes patula, T. erecta*). Yellow, orange, bi-colors. Height: 8–30 inches (20–75cm). Bright discs come as single daisies and double pompons. Good companion plant for vegetables.

Lobelia (*Lobelia erinus*). Pale and dark blue; also violet, pink, crimson, white. Height: 6 inches (15cm). Traditionally used with alyssum to edge flower beds, but the pretty little asymmetrical flowers are better appreciated in pots or trailing from baskets.

Love-lies-bleeding (*Amaranthus caudatus*). Crimson. Height: 2½–3 feet (75–90cm). Distinctive chenille tassels that are good as cut and dried flowers. Keep soil moist.

Petunia (*Petunia* x *hybrida*). Purples, white, reds, pinks, yellows, mottled, striped. Height: 8–16 inches (20–40cm). Upright, spreading, and trailing varieties produce showy trumpets, popular in baskets. Deadhead regularly.

Snapdragon (*Antirrhinum majus*). White, yellow, orange, pink, deep red. Height: 6–24 inches (15–60cm). Velvety spikes of "snapping" flowers. Like sun and very well-drained soil.

Sweet pea (*Lathyrus odoratus*). Pinks, mauves, scarlet, deep purple, white. Height: 6–8 feet (2–2.5m). The butterfly-delicate flowers include bi-colored, veined and frilled versions; make sure you choose a well-scented variety. Soak seeds before sowing and provide a climbing trellis.

Tobacco plant (*Nicotiana* spp.) Greenish, yellow, pink, white, dark red. Height: 1–3 feet (30–90cm). Fragrant, starry flowers open early evening and at night. Most effective in a group. Can withstand a little frost.

Biennials

These are usually sown in late spring or early summer, and then transplanted to a nursery bed and planted out in the fall, ready to flower the following year. To winter outside they should be well established before the cold weather sets in.

Canterbury bell (*Campanula medium*). Blue, white. Height: 2 1/2 feet. (75cm). Pretty bells dangle from a slender, almost leafless spike rising from a rosette of foliage.

Evening primrose (*Oenothera biennis*). * Yellow. Height: 3–5 feet. (1–1.5m). Large cup-shaped flowers open in late afternoon and evening toward the end of summer. Should naturalize if planted in full sun in light, even stony soil.

Forget-me-not (*Myosotis sylvatica*). * Blue; also pink, white variations. Height: 6–12 inches (15–30cm). Creates a pretty sky blue haze over the ground in late spring if planted in bold swathes. Does well in poor soil, even between paving.

Foxglove (*Digitalis purpurea*). * Purples, white. Height: 5 feet. (1.5m). Spires of tubular bells with spotted throats in early summer. Colonizes dappled woodland in the wild, so damp part-shade among shrubs is ideal. Attracts bees and insects. Poisonous.

Hollyhock (*Alcea rosea*). White, yellow, peach, pink, crimson, near-black. Height: 5–6 feet. (1.5–2m). Towering spires of saucer-shaped flowers, associated with the cottage garden. Double versions less appealing. May need staking if not supported by neighboring plants.

Honesty (*Lunaria annua*). * Lilac, white. Height: 2 feet. (60cm). Simple spring flowers, but best known for its silvery seedpods like translucent coins. Sow *in situ* (it does not transplant well) in late spring to flower a year later. Prefers partial shade and attracts early butterflies. Dry seedpods as decoration but leave some for winter beauty.

Pansy (*Viola* x *wittrockiana*). Blue, white, yellow, orange, mahogany, purple, bi-colors. Height: 6–8 inches (15–20cm). Appealing open "faces" on many types. Flourishes in a humus-rich, moist but well-drained soil. Sow fall and winter varieties in early spring.

Sweet William (*Dianthus barbatus*). Purples, pinks, white. Height: 2 feet. (60cm). Dense flowerheads in early summer have a powerful fragrance. Best on neutral to alkaline soil.

Wallflower (*Cheiranthus cheiri*). Yellow, orange, red, stained whites. Height: 10–30 inches (25–75cm). Brings rich velvety colors to the border. Best on an alkaline or neutral soil that is not too fertile.

Perennials

Perennials come up year after year. The traditional herbaceous perennial border was a marvelous sight, but it took up a lot of space and time, and would leave the bed bare and uninteresting during winter. The variety and versatility of perennials, however, mean they can be used not only in modern mixed borders but also in containers and as groundcover. Although soft-stemmed perennials retreat into dormancy, there are also many, such as bergenias, garden pinks, hellebores, and saxifage, that retain some greenery all year in warm climates.

Planting

Container-grown perennials can be planted out at any time, except when the ground is frozen or the weather very hot and dry. The best time for this, however, is the fall, when the soil is still warm. Alternatively, plant in spring, which may be a better idea on heavy soils. Prepare the planting area by turning the soil over as suggested on page 22.

When buying container-grown plants, check that the plant looks healthy, that the crown has strong new shoots and that the soil surface is not covered in algae or too many weeds. The plant should be neither waterlogged nor so dry that the rootball has shrunk away from the pot. Check that the roots are strong and well grown. If the plant is dormant, check that the crown is firm and undamaged and that the soil is moist.

If you have to store bare-rooted, dormant plants for a few days, water the roots and then pack damp compost around them. Wrap them and leave them in a shady spot, away from drying winds.

When planting a whole new bed, start from the back of the border or the middle of an island bed. Walk on the soil as little as possible to avoid compaction, and use wooden boards to cross heavy, wet soil. If you have drawn a plan, mark it out on the soil with a stick or lines of sand, or place container plants in position before you dig any holes. Check that you have left enough room for growth, and that the relative heights of the plants work together. When planting small groundcover or spreading perennials, plant two or three together in a clump to encourage good, dense cover.

Planting perennials

For small plants, use a trowel to dig out a hole in the earth slightly deeper and wider than the rootball of container plants or the roots of a bare-rooted plant. Put the soil from the hole to one side. Sprinkle a slow-release fertilizer like bonemeal, around the sides and base. Place the plant upright in the center of the hole with the top of the compost or the line between stem and root on the same level as the top of the hole. Hold the plant upright with one hand and spread the roots out of bare-rooted specimens. For container-grown plants, loosen the soil at the bottom. With your other hand, fill the soil back into the hole around the plant. Firm in the plant with your fingers or the back of a trowel. Loosen the soil surface and water so that it floods once and drains away. This will prevent the formulation of air bubbles.

For larger plants, dig the planting hole with a spade, placing the earth to one side. The slow release fertilizer can be sprinkled over this pile so it mixes with it when it is put back into the hole. To firm the plant in, tread the ground around the stems without damaging shoots. Tread firmly but not heavily. Loosen the surface of the soil and water as above.

Deadheading

Unless you want to save the seed, remove faded flowers to encourage further flowering. Cutting flowers for the house will have the same benefit—dahlias are particularly well-known as "cut and come again" flowers.

Aftercare

Make sure that new plants do not dry out, but don't just water indiscriminately.

Weed constantly when plants are small (be careful of new herbaceous shoots coming through) and they will later smother much weed growth themselves. Be vigilant against grass growing through mound-forming or groundcover plants. Replace weeds with other plants rather than leaving the earth bare.

Provide large and top-heavy perennials with support before they need it. Twiggy branches pushed into the ground and their tops bent over will give naturalistic supports to smaller plants, but canes and string or wire mesh may be needed for other larger plants. Supports should be almost invisible once the foliage has grown up.

Cutting down dead top growth is a job conventionally done in fall, but any time before the following spring is good. The border can look beautiful with drying seedheads, but ultimately the old stems can get in the way of new growth.

On established beds loosen the topsoil with a fork in fall and follow this in spring with a mulch of well-rotted compost and perhaps a slow-release fertilizer such as blood, fish, and bone. Liquid fertilizer during the growing season tends to encourage leafy growth and weed competition, but will provide nutrients until the soil structure can be improved.

Propagating

Perennials can be propagated by cuttings and division as well as by seed.

Fall is the time to divide plants. Even if you don't want more, plants that are overcrowded or have become woody and non-productive in

Foliage plants
Don't forget the importance of foliage. It lasts much longer than flowers and can bring silver, gold bronze and purple as well as green to a planting. Some, such as acanthus, hostas and macleayas, are even more striking than their blooms.

the center will benefit from being split and replanted. Small perennials can be dug up and pulled apart by hand; larger clumps will need to be levered apart with forks.

Dividing perennials

Lever them out with a fork or, if very large, dig around the plant, then dig under and out with a spade. Place the plant on a firm surface. Put two forks into the plant with their backs to each other. Pull the handles apart and this should give you two plants. You can do it again to divide it further.

Overwintering tender perennials

Perennials such as osteopermums, pelargoniums and salvia species will probably be killed by frost if they are left unprotected through the winter. In mild areas or with plants of borderline hardiness, protect the crowns with dry leaves. Alternatively dig the plants up and overwinter them somewhere frost-free or take cuttings. (Verbena hybrids are easiest propagated by seed.) Tuberous-rooted perennials such as begonias and dahlias can be stored in boxes of almost-dry compost or sand. They should be inspected every few weeks for mold or disease, which should be cut out and the wound dusted with flowers of sulphur.

The right plant in the right place

Since there are perennials to suit almost any situation, make life easy by choosing ones that will relish your soil conditions. Those that perform their best in really damp soil include

hostas, feathery astilbes, ligularias with lofty golden daisy flowers, and the graceful water irises.

Lovers of hot, dry conditions include silver-leaved artemisias, spiky blue-flushed eryngiums, verbascums, and many ornamental grasses, which retain a fountain of colorful leaves all year.

SEEDS

Hardy perennials

Here are some of the huge range of reliable, unfussy perennials. Unless otherwise indicated, all thrive in reasonably fertile, well-drained soil in full sun or partial shade. E = winter green in warm climates.

Bloody cranesbill (*Geranium sanguineum*). Summer. Height: 10–12 inches (25–30cm). Bright magenta-pink flowers on dense, spreading clumps of dark leaves with good fall color. Easy and drought-tolerant.

Delphinium (*Delphinium* spp.) High summer. Height: 5–6 feet (1.5–2m). Elegant spires of blue, pink, white or violet, good for cutting. Needs rich soil and staking well.

Lady's mantle (*Alchemilla mollis*). Early summer–early fall. Height: 1–2 feet (30–60cm). Hazy greenish-yellow flowers and clumps of soft, scalloped leaves. Self-seeds easily. Cut back after flowering to encourage fresh foliage. Can withstand dry conditions.

Lenten rose (*Helleborus orientalis*) E. Mid-winter–late spring. Height: 18 inches (45cm). Cut back overwintering leaves to reveal subtly colored greenish-white, yellow, pink, or purplish flowers. Prefers dappled shade and a slightly damp soil. Good for color and shape during winter.

Lupin (*Lupinus* spp.) Early–mid summer. Height: 3 feet (90cm). Spikes of pea-like flowers in many colors, including bi-colors. Prefers sandy, slightly acid soil.

Red hot poker (*Kniphofia* x *praecox*) E. High summer fall. Height: 1½–4 feet (50–120 cm). Name comes from red and yellow flower spike (although colors range from lime to

terracotta). Prefers fertile soil but abhors winter wet. Tolerates wind and salt. Shelter young plants.

Shasta daisy (*Leucanthemum* x *superbum*). Summer. Height: 3 feet (90cm). Large white daisies on tall stems. Tough and forms large clumps. Good for cutting.

Spurge (*Euphorbia characias*) E. Spring. Height: 3–5 feet. (1–1.5m). Yellow flower-like bracts and handsome blue-gray leaves. Cut off stems after flowering to prevent self-seeding of invasive varieties.

Valerian (*Centranthus ruber*). Early summer –mid fall. Height: 2 feet. (60cm). Clusters of small pink flowers above gray-green foliage. Prefers alkaline soil in full sun.

Yarrow (*Achillea* spp.) E (some). Summer. Height: 8–12 inches (20–30cm). Flat heads of tiny flowers, usually yellow, and ferny green or gray foliage. Good for hot, dry site. Attracts beneficial insects.

Pint-sized perennials

Perennials that form low clumps are particularly suited to rocky places. As well as the well-known aubrieta, dwarf campanulas, saxifrages and stonecrops, try some of the following in paving, rockeries or gravel gardens. All are winter green in warm climates.

Arenaria Spring. Carpet of white flowers.

Dwarf achillea Silvery leaves and cream or pale yellow flowerheads.

Dwarf phlox Spring. Very floriferous, many shades of pink, red and mauve.

Violas For damp shade; little pansy flowers in spring.

Bulbs

Spring bulbs bring color and life to the garden before many shrubs and perennials have begun to stir. Summer bloomers include the spectacular lilies, after which there are fall crocuses and cyclamens to look forward to.

Bulb planter

This is a special tool with a spade-like handle over a metal cylinder which, when pushed into the earth, cuts out a core of grass and earth. Into this, the bulb is dropped and the core, once it is replaced on top, shows little disturbance to the grass.

Spring–early summer

Bulbs are graded by size; the bigger the bulb the bigger the plant. Daffodils are also graded by "noses" or growing points. As each growing point could produce a flower, multi-nosed bulbs are more expensive. Bags of mixed varieties are a mixture of grades as well as types.

Bulbs for all seasons
Plants that produce bulbs or other storage organs become dormant at some time of year. This allows them to be sold "dry."

flower	dormant	buy and plant
spring–early summer	summer	fall
late summer	fall	spring
fall	early summer	late summer

The exception are snowdrops, which are best planted before they die down. Buy them or transplant them "in the green," soon after flowering.

Make sure that bulbs are firm and dry—avoid any that are soft or shrunken. Most can be stored while dry in a cool room or shed.

As well as the myriad crocuses, narcissi, and tulips, many other beautiful bulbs flower at this time of the year. Alliums, the ornamental onions, vary from 6 inches to 4 feet (15–120 cm) or more but all have the characteristic globe-like heads followed by spiky seedheads. They come in almost every color and bloom in late spring or early summer.

The snake's head fritillary (*Fritillaria meleagris*) has a distinctive purplish checkered patterning on its nodding bells and naturalizes well in damp grass. Among its many relations is the appropriately named *F. imperialis*, which stands nearly 3 feet. (1m) tall, topped by a ruff of richly colored orange or yellow bells.

Naturalizing

Crocuses and narcissi naturalize well in grass. Delay cutting until six weeks after the flowers have faded so that the goodness in the leaves can return to the bulb. Tulips look lovely in a meadow, but may only last a couple of years, especially in heavy soil.

Blue scillas and grape hyacinths will spread prolifically and can carpet the ground beneath taller plants. They appreciate the free drainage of a rock garden.

Summer to fall

Queen of the summer bulbs is the gorgeous, often fragrant lily. Lilies require a

humus-rich but well-drained soil, preferably slightly acidic. Plant them deep, with their roots in the shade and sun on their flowers, and feed well.

Most later bulbs are less hardy. Gladioli (also graded by size) will often survive winter with a little protection, as will clivias and eucomis in a dry, sheltered site. A covering of chopped straw will help. For other tender bulbs allow the foliage to die down for as long as possible but lift before the weather grows too wet and cold. Dry and store in brown paper bags or hang in nets.

Hardy fall bulbs include the deceptively delicate little hardy cyclamen (which can also appear in late winter), fall crocuses, and their larger relations, colchicums.

Planting

As a rough guide, plant bulbs twice as deep as their own depth. Set the bulbs out on the surface first, in naturalistic drifts. On wet, heavy soil, add a bed of gravel to the bottom of each hole. A special bulb planter is useful for planting into grass (see page 54).

Bulbs also grow well in pots, bringing early color to containers or as a bright focus for bare parts of the garden.

If you need the space, lift the bulbs after flowering and "heel" them (lay in a shallow depression and cover with soil) in a shady, undisturbed part of the garden until the foliage has died. Then lift them and store, hanging in a net or wrapped in newspaper in a dry place.

Bulb	Depth from top of bulb to soil level	Planting time
Chionodoxa	2in	Fall
Crocus	2in	August–October
Anemone	2in	October–April
Hyacinth	4in	October–November
Gladiolus	4in	March–April
Grape Hyacinth	3in	Fall
Daffodil	4in	August–September
Tulip	4in	October–November
Iris	3in	Fall
Snowdrop	2in	August–September
Bluebell	3in	Fall
Montbretia	2in	March–April
Ranunculus	2in	November–March

Feeding

Bulbs in borders should receive sufficient food in the annual dressing of well-rotted manure or garden compost. If planted in containers they will benefit from liquid fertilizer after flowering and, once the foliage has withered, a mulch of manure or compost. Potash or potassium (see page 12) will encourage good flowers the following year.

Shrubs and trees

Shrubs, and especially trees, are a garden's backbone; they provide a sturdy framework—a permanent setting—for the smaller plants that may come and go. They create a magical mixture of light and shade and bring their own style and character to a garden. They also encourage wildlife into the garden, with shelter for nests, berries for food, and leaf litter for insects to burrow into.

Shrubs range from roses to the seemingly unshrub-like bamboos, from spicy-scented witch hazel (*Hamemelis*) in early spring to the glorious fall shades of euonymus. Some might be termed multi-stemmed trees, while others are only ankle-height. Groundcover shrubs like prostrate junipers, and cotoneasters, and *Pachysandra terminalis* are increasingly popular since, once they are established, they reduce the labor of weeding.

There are shrubs for every exposure, every soil, and every season. Visit parks and gardens open to the public, talk to neighbors, bury yourself in books and magazines and you will soon find yourself overwhelmed by choice. Below are some ideas to help you narrow that choice. In the descriptions E = evergreen; *E* = technically deciduous but retain a presence in winter; * = work well as hedges.

Color in winter and early spring

Evergreens are, of course, the stalwarts of the garden in winter, and conifers in particular come in a wide range of shapes and color variations. There are deciduous shrubs, too, that reveal a new beauty when their leaves fall away. For bright winter stems, *Cornus alba* is a favorite. Cut it right back in spring to within two or three buds of the base or a short main trunk and the new scarlet growth that this promotes will brighten the garden all winter. *Rubus cockburnianus,* an ornamental bramble, provides a forest of arching stems of a startling chalky whiteness. A winter stand of bamboos (*Arundinaria*) can have yellow-striped or purple-black stems as well as vibrant green. They are easy to grow and are uplifting, positive plants that catch and magnify the sound of wind and rain. Some can be invasive, so check carefully the vigor of the variety you are buying. They don't need pruning; just cut older stems to the base in spring to thin overcrowded stands.

There are also shrubs to bring us color in the darkest part of the year:

Mahonia "Charity" Just as most other flowering shrubs are shutting down for the winter, mahonias burst into bloom. This upright shrub has bold, scratchy leaves and impressive thick trails of yellow blooms. Not fussy about soil. Prune only for symmetry.

*Viburnum (*Viburnum tinus*) E. Small white flower clusters stay all winter in warm areas and show up well against dark green foliage. Easy to grow (will tolerate alkaline soils) and regular pruning not required.

Witch hazel (*Hamamelis mollis*). Valued for its yellow spidery flowers that appear on the bare branches and give off a deliciously spicy scent. Grows to about 8 feet (2.5m). Likes neutral to acidic soil and tolerates city air. No pruning necessary.

Forsythia An old garden reliable that is often neglected because it thrives in all sorts of conditions. Flowers vary from soft lemon yellow to brassy free-range egg-yolk. Prune to keep bushes tidy and vigorous.

Japanese quince (*Chaenomeles japonica*) E. Blooms like small saucers in bright oranges, pinks, reds, and white are followed by hard apple-like fruits in summer. Happy in all soils and tolerates shade. Responds well to cutting back hard, but only needs to be pruned to keep within bounds.

Flowering currant (*Ribes sanguineum*). An easy shrub that can grow on a cold, shaded wall. Its little candy-pink racemes of flowers bridge the gap between the remnants of winter and the arrival of "real" spring. Prune to encourage growth.

Flowers in late spring and early summer

There is no shortage of interest in the garden through these months, and the variety is immense. As an illustration, the following three shrubs are all hardy and may all bloom at the same time, but their contribution to the garden couldn't be more different. They also all come in a variety of sizes, so can be suited to different plots.

Broom (*Cytisus* spp.) E. From prostrate shrublets that look good tumbling over small walls to rounded bushes 6–8 feet (2–2.5m) tall. Whippy upright stems (you can see where the name "broom" comes from) are transformed when clothed in clouds of yellow, red-bronze, or cream pea-flowers. They thrive in poor, dry soil. No need to prune except to shape as required.

Mock orange (*Philadelphus* spp.) Rounded shrubs from 3–10 feet (1m to 3m). with abundant white blooms. Heavily fragrant. There are double as well as single types, and also some with golden or variegated leaves. Likes all soils and will adapt to pollution and salt. To renew, cut overgrown shrubs to 1 foot. (30cm) above ground in early spring.

Rhododendrons E. Includes small, neat-leaved domes to large, spreading shrubs that will grow tree-like in time. Almost every flower color from white and yellow to pink, lilac, and scarlet, in clusters from little posies to almost the size of a football. Happy in shade but require an acid soil. Among azaleas, which are part of the same family, yellows, salmons, and oranges predominate and some have a heady, honeyed fragrance. Many azaleas are deciduous, with rich fall colors. Pruning seldom necessary.

Added attractions

With so many possibilities, why not choose shrubs that have attractions beyond good foliage and flowers? Fleshy hips from roses such as *Rosa rugosa* and the hard fruits of Japanese quince (also known as japonica) make delicious jellies. Lavenders, shrubby herbs, and buddleia are all magnets for butterflies, while bees flock to these and numerous others, including berberis, cotoneasters, elaeagnus, viburnums and hebes. Berried shrubs will attract birds, which in turn will help keep down the pest population.

Classic shrubs for fragrance

buddleia

choisya

lavender (*Lavandula* spp.)

lilac (*Syringa* spp.)

mock orange (*Philadelphus*)

roses

Christmas box (*Sarcococcus humilis*)

viburnums

Late season color

Berberis and pyracantha are popular choices for fall berries, and rightly so—they are easy, accommodating evergreens, happy to be trained up walls or cut back hard as hedges. A pyrachantha's berry clusters are more showy, but berberis berries come in purple and black as well as orange, red, and yellow. Pyracantha flowers in creamy clusters, while berberis has small blooms of orange or yellow.

Other reliable berry shrubs are cotoneasters, which range from groundcovers to tall shrubs. All give a spectacular display accompanied by rich foliage colors (some types are at least partially evergreen). The late spring flowers are creamy-white or pale pink. These will all attract bees and birds.

As well as berries, make the most of colored leaves and late bursts of flower:

Butterfly bush (*Buddleia davidii*) E. Honey-scented flowerheads in lilac, purple, or white last well into the fall. Cut back to a low permanent framework early each spring, to encourage fresh growth and more flowers.

Fuchsia The crimson, pink and purple, or pink and white flowers hang like fairy lights and get better as the fall progresses. Plant in fertile, moist soil. Technically evergreen, but except in mild areas, where they make good informal hedges, fuchsias are inclined to die back and re-sprout from base in spring.

Guelder rose (*Viburnum opulus*). Foliage like small vine leaves turns to fire to vie with the clusters of scarlet or yellow berries.

Heather (*Erica & Calluna spp.*) E. Species of these low, hummocky shrubs flower at different times throughout the year. Color varies from white to lilac to deep crimson, and many of the fall-flowering *Calluna vulgaris* have bright golden, silvery or foxy-bronze foliage. They like a sunny position and most require an acid soil, although some *Erica* species will tolerate chalk.

Hebe (Autumn Glory) E. Small erect shrub with small cones of purple-blue flowers right through the summer to early winter.

Likes all soils, but is best sheltered from cold winds. No pruning required.

***Rosa rugosa** A vigorous, dense, and prickly shrub. The single magenta or white flowers are large and showy, and late ones are joined by fat round hips the size and color of cherry tomatoes.

***Shrubby cinquefoil** (*Potentilla* spp.) E. These broad, rounded shrubs begin flowering in late spring, but are still putting on a good show right at the end of fall. The buttercup-like flowers range from white and pale yellow through to gold, salmon, and tomato red. Hardy in all areas, but prefers a well-drained soil and sunny position.

***St John's Wort** (*Hypericum* "Hidcote") E. Medium-sized, dense, rounded shrub with glowing golden flowers and pointed red seed capsules through late summer and fall. Tolerates dry soils and grows well in chalk. Cut back hard in spring.

Spindle bush (*Euonymus europaeus*). Glorious medley of fall colors as leaves turn bright pink and red and the dangling scarlet fruits burst open to reveal orange seeds. Ultimately very tall and can be grown on a single trunk, as a tree.

Wall shrubs often keep providing color later than those in the open garden.

Notable foliage

Since the flowers are a passing attraction, it is worth paying attention to the foliage of your shrubs, as this contributes to the garden for a much longer period of time. In addition to different shapes and textures, look out for those with variegated leaves, or leaves flushed with gold or purple.

Silver-leaved shrubs usually do best on dryish soil in full sun; they are often a good choice for a coastal location. *Senecio* (E) is particularly showy, making a mound of white-felted leaves. Its yellow daisy flowers are a very secondary attraction.

Osmanthus heterophyllus (E) is an anomaly —a quiet shrub that attracts attention. Many people mistake it for a holly—and are then surprised by the fragrant flowers in late summer. Requires protection from cold winds. *Aureomarginatus* has yellow-margined leaves.

Good for coastal situations

****Elaeagnus* spp.** E. The yellow-splashed foliage of *E. pungens* "Maculata" cheers wintry borders, while *E. ebbingei* has evergreen down-covered leaves and *E. commutata* has deciduous silvery leaves and berries.

****Escallonia rubra* var. *macrantha*** E. Vigorous, rounded shrub with bright pink-red tubular flowers from summer to early fall. Not suitable for heavy, wet soils and best grown as a wall shrub in cold inland areas.

****Griselinia littoralis*** E. Less hardy inland, but the leathery variegated leaves make good screens in coastal areas. Grows purple fruits in fall if plants of both sexes are present.

Tamarisk (*Tamarix* spp.) Plumes of pink flowers in late spring followed by feathery foliage give this tall shrub a very light, smoky air. It is hardy in most sunny sites if the soil is not heavy and wet.

Roses

There was a time when a rose bed, lovingly tended, was the pride of nearly every garden. The reward for battles with black spot, rust, and complicated pruning regimes were beautiful blooms and the admiration of the neighbors. Then a certain disillusionment set in: roses were a lot of hard work; new varieties had little scent; the large blooms sat awkwardly in mixed beds. Now, the wheel has turned and we have the best of both worlds: greater choice and a simpler approach.

The rose family is huge, with a great deal of interbreeding and confusing names.

Species roses and old hybrids typically make large, beautifully scented shrubs that only flower once a year, but they vary from "Max Graf", a clear pink single flower that makes good groundcover, to the repeat-flowering, blush pink buttons of "Cecile Brunner". Most are tough and unfussy about soil and some, like the rugosas, are naturally disease-resistant. Others are susceptible to mildews and rusts.

Breeding for larger and more elegant flowers, repeat or continuous flowering, and new colors led to bush roses: hybrid teas (sometimes called large-flowered), floribundas (or cluster-flowered), polyanthas and many more. This gave us some excellent roses that bloomed over a long period, but also some stiff, gawky plants that had lost their fragrance. These highly bred types are the most demanding in terms of care and conditions, and dislike competition at root level, so are best suited to growing in a dedicated bed. A new generation of hybrids combines the best of the old and the new.

Roses with labels such as "patio," "miniature," or "groundcover" are just small or spreading types. Standard roses are bushes grafted onto bare stems—a groundcover rose on a stem makes a weeping standard.

Plant roses in an open, sunny site in winter or early spring (better for clay soils). They prefer a fertile, moisture-retentive soil but will cope with a wide range of soils if plenty of humus is added. Prepare a deep hole and add well-rotted garden compost or manure, with a sprinkling of bonemeal. Cut back hybrid teas and floribundas hard after planting, to the second or third outward-facing bud.

Deadhead to promote more flowers, but leave those varieties which have decorative hips in fall. Before buds start to grow in spring, remove fallen leaves, burn or destroy if they are diseased, and mulch with well-rotted compost, keeping it away from stems to avoid "burning". Remove suckers. If a rose should die, choose a new site for a replacement, to avoid a build-up of soil-borne diseases (replant sickness).

Pruning roses
♦ Prune when roses are dormant.
♦ Always cut to an outward-facing bud.
♦ Take out the three Ds (see page 71).
♦ Aim to open out the inside of the bush to help air circulate.
♦ Hard pruning will result in fewer but larger flowers and is more appropriate to bush roses; take them down to half or even a quarter of their height.
♦ Leave shrub roses unpruned for the first few years and then prune repeat-flowering ones by one-third to half their height. Prune once-flowering types lightly, if at all. Large shrub roses can be cut back hard if they have gotten out of hand.
♦ Cut out one or two stems of old shrub roses each year to encourage new growth.

Planting shrubs
Container-grown plants can be planted at almost any time unless the ground is frozen or the weather very hot and dry. The ideal time is during their dormant season, between late fall and early spring, so that they can settle in through the summer before the cold weather arrives again.

Bare-rooted specimens are dug from the nursery while they are dormant, and it is important to get them into the ground as soon as possible. If the weather makes this impossible they will last a few days in a frost-free place, wrapped in plastic to keep the roots moist.

Some shrubs are shipped rootballed, the roots are covered with peat moss and wrapped in netting and burlap or plastic. Plant these in the warmer months of spring or fall. They can be left longer before planting but it is difficult to water them without undoing the rootball. When planting, take off the netting and other coverings or they will restrict root growth and strangle the plant.

Make sure the planting hole is large enough to easily accomodate the roots, and provide a good start for these long-term plants with some well-rotted garden compost or manure mixed into the soil. On very wet soils, mix in some sand or multi-purpose compost (or your own well-rotted bulky organic soil conditioner) and on sandy soils add a bulky soil conditioner to help retain moisture. Backfill around the shrub with the enriched soil and firm down well. Water well; add at least a bucketful and spread 4 inches (10cm) of moist hay, straw, leaf, or grass mulch, as a weed suppressant and for moisture retention.

Shrubs transplanted in summer will survive better if they have fewer leaves through which to lose water. Trimming back the leaves will help, and an effective but more brutal treatment is to cut the whole shrub back to 6 inches (15cm) above the ground, or to the second or third bud above ground if this is where new growth will come from.

Care and maintenance
Until established, give shrubs a good soaking at least once a week, maybe twice during dry weather. Direct the hose at the roots.

The main maintenance for shrubs is pruning (see page 71). Shrubs being shaped or hard-pruned to increase flower and berry production will need an application of well-rotted compost, manure, or top dressing of organic fertilizer each spring.

Trees

Trees make a healthy contribution to our environment. Because of their size their emits of oxygen and absorption of carbon dioxide is much greater than from other plants. Like an old building, a mature tree has seen and withstood far more than the everyday problems of our own lives. This gives comfort and faith in the future, so planting trees is a wonderfully optimistic process.

Once established, trees require little maintenance, but their very permanence means it is worth thinking about what is right for your garden.

Size

An over-dominant tree or one too close to the house, where its roots will become a danger to the foundations and watercourses, is a liability. The recommended minimum planting distance from a building for an oak or poplar, for instance, is 40 feet (12m). If you have the space, then think long-term and plant one or more large trees—they may take a while to grow to maturity but you will have a protective and proprietorial interest in their progress.

For small gardens

None of the following trees grow taller than 25 feet (7–8m), and all have more than one season of interest.

Amelanchier Pretty blossom-like flowers in mid-spring are followed by small red fruits. Good fall color. Often grows multi-stemmed.

*Hawthorn "Paul's Scarlet"** (*Crataegus laevigata*). Compact shape, thorny with dark pink flowers in spring and red berries in fall.

Crabapple (*Malus* x *arnoldiana*). Many crabs make lovely small trees. This one is arching, with fragrant pink flowers fading to white followed by red-yellow fruit.

Cornelian cherry (*Cornus mas*). Twiggy and shrub-like, with masses of tiny yellow flowers before the leaves. Good fall color.

Ornamental pear (*Pyrus salicifolia*). A semi-weeping dome of silver leaves studded with creamy white flowers in spring.

Catalpa "Aurea" (*Catalpa bignonioides*). Potentially quite large, but hard pruning not only keeps the catalpa small but makes its large heart-shaped leaves grow huge. Slender "beans" dangling from the tree in fall enhance the exotic appearance.

Shape and shadow

Some trees have a dense canopy when in full leaf, while others give just dappled shade. Check on the direction your new tree will be casting its shadow, and consider if in time this will deprive other plants of light.

Trees come in many shapes. Look for columnar (like a cigar), cones, wide-based pyramids, round-headed bushy, open-tiered (like a cake tray), weeping (drooping or trailing branches), prostrate (spreading out close to the ground), globular, flat-topped tiered (horizontal branches like a cedar tree) and small round-top tiered (like a mushroom).

Trees with narrow profiles or light canopies

These are also suitable for a small garden.

Flowering cherry (*Prunus* spp.) One with

a broad outline will give you an attractive, spreading shape without a heavy shadow. A gorgeous froth of blossom and fiery fall coloring are added bonuses.

Mountain ash (*Sorbus* spp.) Frond-like leaves give a light, ferny appearance to these small trees. Great fall color highlighted by berry clusters (mostly orange/red, but white on *S. cashmiriana* and pink on *S. vilmorinii*).

Conifers Narrow columnar shapes abound—one of the very slimmest is the stately blue-grey *Juniperus virginiana* "Skyrocket".

Silver birch (*Betula pendula*). Such light, airy trees that a small group will take up little room and make a feature of the silvery peeling bark. Prefers a light, sandy soil.

Black locust (False acacia) (*Robinia pseudoacacia* "Frisia"). Tall and graceful, with fluttering golden-green leaflets. Avoid windy sites because branches are brittle.

Judas tree (*Cercis siliquastrum*). A very open tree whose purple pea flowers burst in late spring from every part of the tree, even the trunk. Can be multi-stemmed. Slow-growing and prefers alkaline conditions.

Color

Leaf color and shape, seasonal flowers, and fruit all contribute to a tree's beauty and presence. You may also like to consider, if a tree is deciduous (sheds its leaves in fall), any winter attributes such as interesting bark or strong outline.

Cherry plum (*Prunus cerasifera*). Pink blossom in early spring followed by black-purple leaves. A handsome tree.

Paperbark maple (*Acer griseum*). Slow-growing and spreading tree, with ornately peeling bark and brilliant red and orange fall color. Plant in an open and sunny position.

Corkscrew hazel (*Corylus avellana* "Contorta"). Small, with twisted branches that are especially impressive in the winter. Yellow catkins form in early spring.

*Holly (*Ilex aquifolium*). Foliage comes in a variety of spiky forms, also variegated. Requires tree of opposite gender nearby to produce berries. Withstands pollution.

Smokebush (Royal Purple) (*Cotinus coggygria*). Plum-purple foliage turns bright red in fall. Hazy heads of tiny flowers give a smoky appearance.

Planting and staking

Planting a tree is much the same as planting a shrub. Container-grown conifers often fare better than bare-rooted ones, because they do not always like to be transplanted. The younger a tree is the easier it is to get it established. A mature tree looks good right away, but will need more care and can be slow to grow for a few years after planting. It will also be much more expensive.

If a tree trunk's bark is nibbled all round so there is no continuous line of bark to transfer nutrients, it will die (although immediately applying tar or paint will help vigorous varieties,) so guard against rabbits and deer.

To plant trees, skim the turf off the area and set aside. Dig a circular or square hole 2 feet (60cm) deep and 2 feet (60cm) wide. Check to see how the roots fit in the hole with the soil line where it was last planted level with the ground. As necessary, dig more earth out, tailoring the hole to make the roots fit. If it is impossible to dig the hole larger or deeper, cut the roots to fit. If there are any broken roots, cut them off. Put the turf upside down in the hole and sprinkle bonemeal over and around the edges. If there is no turf then add a good layer of well-rotted garden compost or manure, mixed in with a bit of soil.

On clay or waterlogged soil break down any clods of earth you have dug out, and mix with sand or multi-purpose compost. On sandy soils add soil conditioner to help moisture retention.

Staking is not done to hold a tree up, but to prevent its roots from being disturbed when the tree moves in the wind. It should only be

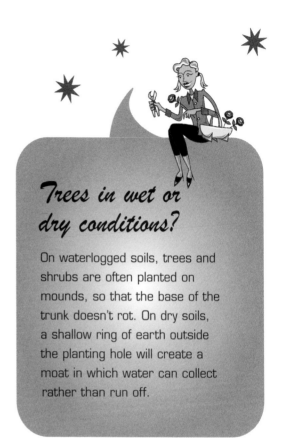

Trees in wet or dry conditions?

On waterlogged soils, trees and shrubs are often planted on mounds, so that the base of the trunk doesn't rot. On dry soils, a shallow ring of earth outside the planting hole will create a moat in which water can collect rather than run off.

necessary until the roots have grown to firmly anchor the tree. Traditionally, tall stakes have been used, but nowadays a low stake is preferred. A low stake will come about a third of the way up the trunk. This will allow movement in the upper tree which will help to stimulate the roots to grow down both quicker and stronger.

The stake is placed on the windward side, so the wind blows the tree away from it. Place the stake off-center in the hole, and drive in until firm. Set the tree, with roots spread out, as close to the stake and vertical. Check that

the soil line on the trunk is level with the ground because the tree will grow better at this depth.

Fill the hole half-full to cover the roots, and tread down very gently. Fill the rest of the hole to the surface and tread down more firmly this time. Fill the remaining soil so that the surface is even with the ground level.

Tie two planting ties, one at the top of the stake and the other half-way down. Use spacers between trunk and stake so the trunk doesn't rub against the stake.

Planting small trees and shrubs from containers or with rootballs is the same as the above except that the soil around the roots is disturbed as little as possible. The hole can be smaller depending on the size of the pot or rootball, but it must still be roomy enough for the plant to sit comfortably within it and leave enough space to fill up with good soil if the earth is poor.

Staking is different from that of the bare-rooted plant, in that the stake is prevented from going through the rootball by being put in diagonally after planting. The stake is driven into the soil on the side away from the prevailing wind, so that as the wind blows the tree will be pushed against the stake and not blown over. The stake is tied, with a spacer, where it crosses the tree trunk and is adjusted as the trunk grows and it becomes too tight.

Care and maintenance

♦ Keep newly planted trees well watered. With larger trees, a half-buried hollow pipe will ensure water gets down to the bottom roots. Set it outside the root ball to avoid problems.

♦ Check tree ties once a year and loosen them before they become too tight and inhibit the flow of sap. A large specimen tree may need to be staked for up to five years, but stakes on most trees can be removed after a couple of years.

♦ Keep the surface around the tree free of weeds (and grass for the first few years). Top up mulches or use a biodegradable tree mat of wool, thick newspaper, or carpet.

Conifers

The most important consideration when buying a conifer is its eventual size. Many grow slowly but surely into giants—and of course, some grow quickly into giants, like x *Cupressocyparis leylandii* (see page 80). There are natural dwarfs but many sold as suitable for rock gardens or containers are just young versions of slow-growing, full-sized trees.

Unlike most deciduous trees, you cannot control size by pruning. Yew, juniper, and red cedar (*thuja spp.*) can be clipped for hedging, but specimen varieties of red cedar can take years to recover from a slight trim and mature wood will not regenerate. Only dead branches or green growth on a golden or variegated variety should be cut out.

The magic of pruning

Pruning helps to keep woody plants healthy, vigorous and decorative. Some plants, such as hedges and trained wall shrubs, will need regular care, while most will need only minor maintenance.

Pruning tools

Before pruning, consider your tools.

Secateurs A good pair may be expensive but will be stronger and last longer. Scissor and hammer actions each have their devotees, so try both. Make sure that the blades open wide—you want to be able to cut stems up to at least ¹/₂ inch (1cm) in diameter. Position the stem in the throat of the blades so that all the blade is used rather than the tips, which will cause strain.

Pruning saw This is useful for taking out larger branches. Choose a curved blade with teeth that will saw in both directions as you pull or push.

Long-handled pruner Useful for getting at places you can't reach with the secateurs, and will cut larger branches.

Shears For clipping hedges and trimming some woody plants and herbs.

Leather gardening gloves will protect your hands from thorny or rough branches.

The three Ds—dead, diseased or damaged

Growth that is dead, diseased, or damaged is bad for the health of the plant and therefore must be the first to go. Another D could be added to these: dangerous. Is there a branch that is too low or likely to poke out an eye? The three (or four) Ds should be dealt with irrespective of the type of tree of shrub.

On the whole the harder a shoot is pruned, the more vigorously it will grow. This may be what you require—or it may not. It can cause more work each year to cut the new growth away again. Be wary, therefore, of giving a "haircut" (cutting all stems to the same length) to plants other than hedges, topiary specimens, or particular shrubs that respond well to this treatment.

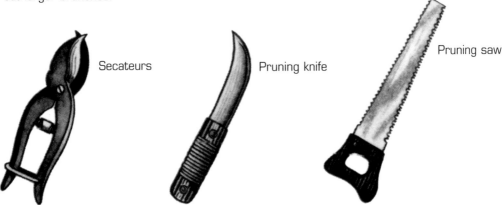

Secateurs

Pruning knife

Pruning saw

Good circulation

Think of the circulation of sap as being like our own blood circulation. If there are tight angles to negotiate, the sap becomes sluggish and slows down. A plant also relies on the circulation of the outer elements—air and light. Congested or crossing branches reduce airflow, increasing humidity and promoting fungus or mildew. Prune to open up the system so it flows more easily.

Timing

When you prune can make a big difference. Prune plants that bleed (leak sap) while dormant in winter. Evergreens are best pruned in mid-spring to leave the cuts less vulnerable to frost.

Timing is also important for flowers (which in turn may generate fruits, nuts, or berries). Prune all the new stems off a shrub that flowers on new wood and you will lose a season's flowers. Encourage too much new growth on a shrub that produces on older wood and it will not have the energy for a good display. The general rule is to prune after flowering if plants bloom before midsummer, or in early spring if they flower after midsummer.

Types of pruning

Although the principles of pruning remain the same for all woody plants, fruit trees and bushes are a special case and are dealt with in their own chapter (see pages 106–121).

Pruning cuts

Different pruning techniques are used according to whether a plant produces buds alternately or opposite each other. With alternate buds, angle the pruning cut across a stem, just above a bud and in the same direction the bud is growing. With opposite growing buds, cut straight across the stem above a strongly growing pair of buds. When cutting, try to make a clean, definite cut. This is because cuts with ragged edges can be slow to heal. Use secateurs for cutting stems up to half an inch (1cm) in diameter and use a pruning saw or long-handled pruners or loppers for larger branches.

Clipping

This is the simplest way to tidy straggly branches and encourage compact growth. Use shears and just cut all stems back to one height or level; there is no need to look for the right bud. This is what hedges need (see page 81) and also how topiary shapes are trained. Climbing roses can also be treated roughly like this and will bush back bravely. Give shrubby evergreen herbs like lavender and rosemary a "haircut" in mid spring.

A more subtle version of this is to pinch out the soft growing tips with finger and thumb. Herbs benefit from this method and will grow more thickly.

Improving shape

For other trees and shrubs, such indiscriminate cutting promotes unbalanced or over-vigorous growth. Before you start cutting, study where the branches are coming from. Cut them back to the main stem or to the ground if that is how they grow. Use secateurs and a pruning saw and keep standing back to look at how the plant rests in the landscape, what it frames or is framed by. Cut less rather than more.

Pruning for air and sun to circulate

Thinning out the growth also means observing where the branches begin. Getting air and sun into the center of the plant is what you need to achieve, but don't simply take out all the central growth. Do it gradually, be methodical, and pause regularly to consider the result.

Pruning for regeneration

This is taking out old wood to encourage new—a very satisfying form of pruning since there is a lot of cutting without the anxiety of aesthetics and with the knowledge that you are encouraging healthy regrowth. This only applies to certain shrubs and then only the established ones, so allow them three to five years to mature before carrying out any regeneration pruning.

Climbers

Climbing plants give height and variety while taking up little ground space. They will produce stunning flowers or beautiful foliage against walls, up pyramid supports, over pergolas, along fences, or through shrubs and trees.

Climbers through trees and shrubs
Brighten up an early-flowering shrub with a late-flowering climber, or team up contrasting flowers or foliage. Pair suitable climbers with hosts that they will not end up smothering, and ensure that there is enough root room for both plants. The *viticella* and *texensis* types of clematis are an excellent choice in many situations; some are quite vigorous but as they are cut back to grow almost from the base each year, they do not build up a heavy framework of branches.

They will also add maturity to a new house or kindly disguise something you would sooner not see, like a chainlink fence or an ugly expanse of wall.

There are immensely attractive and useful annual and herbaceous perennial climbers, and you can also train bushy shrubs vertically against a wall or fence, but here we are concerned with climbing shrubs.

A climber will either twine its stems or leaf-stems around a support, send out tendrils, or attach itself to a surface with aerial roots or suckers. Self-clingers grow best up a solid surface such as a wall, but tendrils and twining stems will need some sort of wire or trellis framework to hug.

To make a ladder of horizontal wires, use galvanized wire held by vine eyes. The wires can be stretched between free-standing posts (making the base for a "hedge" of

climbers) or across a wall or fence, held
1–2 inches (3–5cm) away from the surface.
Start the first wire about 3 feet (90cm)
from the ground and position the rest at
10–12 inch (25–30cm) intervals.

Trellis is more decorative and can also
be either free-standing or attached to a
wall. Trellis panels can also extend the
height of a boundary wall or fence, to
provide greater privacy while giving climbers
extra height. Be sure to choose a
sturdy construction.

Tying climbers, at least in the early stages,
will start them in the right direction and
encourage reluctant clingers. During the
growing season guide new shoots, tying them
as necessary, and check that previous ties are
not too tight. Always use twine or natural fiber
ties, which a stem's expanding girth can
break; rigid plastic or synthetic twine will cut
into a stem, possibly severing it.

Planting

Prepare the soil as for other shrubs, with
nutritious soil and sufficient drainage. Plant
about 18 inches (45cm) away from a wall, to
avoid the dry rain shadow and to give roots
room to grow. Spread roots away from the
wall and provide a temporary stake to guide
the stems toward the support.

Choosing climbers

The following is just a small selection to give a
taste of the variety of climbers that are
available. All of them are deciduous unless
described otherwise.

Bittersweet (*Celastrus orbiculatus*).
Vigorous twiner to 20–30 feet (6–9m). Showy
yellow berries open to reveal scarlet seeds in
a display that lasts through the winter. Good
fall foliage color. Suitable for cold, shaded wall.
Will grow in any reasonable soil.
Pruning: Cut out weak growth and shorten
stems in early spring, after berries have gone.

Clematis Large, very varied family that
attach with tendrils. (Herbaceous clematis do
not twine and are treated as perennials.) Likes
well-drained, slightly alkaline soil that is rich
and moist; keep plants shaded at the soil level
to keep the roots cool, but in the sun for the
stems and leaves. Plant 2 inches (5cm)
deeper than when in the pot, taking care not
to damage the thin, brittle stems. After
planting, cut back all varieties to a pair of
strong buds about 1 foot (30cm) from the
ground, to encourage bushy growth. Top
dress each spring with a potash-rich mixture
and mulch in summer with well-rotted
compost or manure. Pruning: depends on type.

Small-flowered varieties that bloom in late winter–early spring

Examples: *C. alpina* and *C. macropetala* (both
blue, sometimes pink or white, bells, single
and double); *C. montana* (white or pink; very
vigorous); *C. armandii* (white, scented) and
other winter-flowering evergreens.
Pruning: After flowering, remove any damaged
stems and shorten those that have exceeded
their allotted space. Plants that have become
a tangle of woody stems can be cut back to
2–3 feet (60–90cm) above the ground.

Large-flowered varieties that bloom late spring–early summer and again mid–late summer

Examples: "Nelly Moser" (pale pink-mauve with darker stripe; good in shade); "Lausurstern" (lavender blue); "The President" (deep purple); "Henryi" (white); 'Vyvyan Pennell" (purple double)

Pruning: Remove any damaged stems either in early spring or after flowering; otherwise just lightly trim until plants become too straggly. To regenerate, cut back to lowest pair of strong buds, 2–3 feet (60–90cm) from ground in late winter. This avoids heavy top growth.

Later large- and small-flowered varieties

Examples: *C. orientalis* and *C. tangutica* (both yellow bells); *C. texensis* varieties (little pink or red goblets); *C. viticella* types such as 'Mme Julia Correvon" (bright reddish purple), "Purpurea Plena Elegans" (double violet puffballs); *C. jackmanii* types such as "Ernest Markham" (rich pink), "Perle d'Azur" (sky blue)

Pruning: Every winter cut back to lowest pair of strong buds on each stem. They will put on strong fresh growth in the spring.

Ivy (*Hedera* spp.)

Vigorous, evergreen self-clinger. Familiar climber that can be rampant and troublesome if neglected. There are numerous variegated varieties with neater habits. Will thrive in shade in any soil, but variegated varieties need some sun.

Pruning: Clip each year with sharp shears and watch for shoots growing into window frames or gutters.

Climbing hydrangea (*Hydrangea anomola* subsp. *petiolaris*).

Vigorous to 50 feet (15m); self-clinging but requires tying to begin with. Dark leaves set off large, flat, creamy-white flowerheads in early summer. Plant in cool, shaded position in well-drained fertile soil. Keep moist until established, and give an annual top dressing in spring.

Pruning: Trim back stems that exceed their allotted position.

Honeysuckle (*Lonicera* spp.)

Vigorous to 12–20 feet (4–6m). Will twine up trellis but better trailing from arches, fences or trees. Sweetly scented tubular flowers from yellow to rosy red and purple-flushed bloom throughout summer. *L. "Halliana"* is evergreen with pale yellow flowers. Plant in fertile, moist soil with roots in shade.

Pruning: None except removing dead wood.

Passionflower (*Passiflora caerulea*).

Climbs with tendrils to 20 feet (6m) but can die back to base each winter if not in sheltered spot. Exotic Catherine wheels of blue/white flowers which may be followed by bright orange edible fruits after a warm summer. Choose a sunny, warm site and plant in fertile, free-draining soil in late spring. Apply a top dressing of general fertilizer in late spring if growth is slow.

Pruning: Cut weak or dead shoots in spring and shorten sideshoots to 6 inches (15cm).

Russian vine (mile-a-minute vine) (*Fallopia baldschuanica*).

Rampant twiner, growing 15 feet (5m) per year. Will quickly cover old sheds, dead trees,

or unsightly walls. Hazy white or pink-tinted sprays of flowers in late summer. Plant in spring in any reasonable soil, in sun, or in partial shade.

Pruning: Cut back in spring to keep in check.

Summer jasmine (*Jasminum officinale*). Twining to 25 feet (7–8m,) more in favorable areas. Scented, small white trumpet-like flowers from midsummer to fall. Quick growing but needs warm and sunny site because it can be killed by heavy frosts. Plant in any soil that is not too fertile.

Pruning: Cut out congested stems.

Trumpet vine (*Campsis spp.*; also *Bignonia*) Self-clinger to 25 feet (7–8m), vigorous but not always winter hardy. Bold, brightly colored trumpet flowers in late summer. Plant in fertile soil in sunny, sheltered position. Can also grow in a pot. Keep soil moist, mulch in summer and tie in new stems until established. Flowers attract hummingbirds.

Pruning: Cut back flowered stems in late winter.

Virginia creeper (*Parthenocissus quinquefolia*). Self-clinging, vigorous to 70 feet (20m). Could cover a house, but better as a cover for sheds, rough-barked trees, fences and rubbish areas. Spectacular, flame-tinted leaves in fall. Plant in fertile, moisture-retentive soil.

Pruning: Cut back to maintain. Will not damage sound walls but keep growth below gutters.

Wisteria (*Wisteria sinensis*). Dramatic thick-trunked twiner. Will reach 60 feet (20m). Hardy, but appreciates a little shelter. Pendulous racemes of fragrant

lavender or white flowers in late spring. Buy container plants that are as mature as possible, since wisterias can take a long time to flower. Guide to horizontal wires on walls or over pergolas, from which long flower strands can trail. Plant in fertile, humus-rich soil and top dress each spring with general fertilizer.

Pruning: Reduce current season's growth to 6 inches (15cm) after flowering, then in late winter shorten these and all new shoots to two or three buds from their base to encourage flowering.

Climbing roses

Strictly speaking, these are not climbers at all (except some rampant varieties) but are always thought of as such in the garden. Short "pillar" roses may only grow to 6–8 feet (2–2.5m), while vigorous varieties will spread over a tall wall, reaching 20 feet (6m) or more. Like bush roses, they come in a wide range of styles and colors, from vigorous but once-only salmon-pink "Albertine", to continuous-flowering, disease-resistant "Maigold" and from full-petaled deep scarlet "Ena Harkness" to single "Handel", whose cerise-flushed blooms last through the fall.

After planting cut out any weak stems, and take 3 inches (8cm) from the tips of remaining stems to encourage growth. Mulch with well-rotted compost each spring (but don't let it scorch the stems). Make sure roses planted against walls or up trees get sufficient water.

Because flowers are produced at the ends of shoots, train the main stems as horizontally

as possible, making them produce more shoots, and therefore more flowers.
Pruning: Annually after leaf fall and before spring growth starts. Cut old flowered stems back to the main stem, leaving 2 eyes (potential buds). Always make cuts to just above an outward-pointing bud. On mature plants cut out one or two of the oldest stems near to the ground to avoid congestion and encourage vigorous new growth.

Hedges

A hedge is a natural backdrop to the garden. Deciduous hedges give constant variety with berries, flowers and leaf color, while evergreens provide attractive, living structure all year round. Hedges also filter the wind more effectively than fences. In its favor, you do not have to wait for a fence to grow, and its slim profile takes up less precious room in a small garden. Against these cautions, hedges are a vibrant and lovely part of gardens that will long outlast a fence—a yew hedge can live for 200 years or more.

What to choose

Traditional beech, yew, privet, and holly have retained their popularity so long because they respond well to clipping and have good dense growth. Don't feel, though, that your choice need be limited to these. Hedges are only shrubs or trees that have been planted close together in a row and cut to a certain shape, and many of the trees and shrubs described on pages 58–67 make good hedges. Here are just a few more ideas:

Hedge tapestries can be made by mixing different varieties. A traditional rural mix includes hawthorn, elder, hazel, and wild rose. In the more ornamental garden a mixture of green- and purple-leaved cherry plums (*Prunus cerasifera* and *P. cerasifera* "Atropupurea") makes a good windbreak.

For cold, exposed sites
beech (*Fagus sylvatica*)
hornbeam (*Carpinus betulus*)
Cornus mas, Escallonia, Griselinia littoralis, and *Elaeagnus* all stand up well to salty coastal winds.

Thorny to deter intruders
berberis
blackthorn (*Prunus spinosa*)
hawthorn (*Crataegus monogyna*)
holly (*Ilex* spp.)
rose (*Rosa rugosa*)

Dwarf hedges
For inside the garden, perhaps beside a path or around a herb bed
rosemary (*Rosmarinus officinalis*)
box (*Buxus sempervirens*)
cotton lavender (*Santolina chamaecyparissus*)
lavender (*Lavandula* spp.)
cinquefoil (*Potentilla fruticosa*)

A fedge

Willow can be grown as a "fedge" or living screen. Fresh willow branches pushed into the ground during winter will begin to root and in spring will send out long, whippy, new stems that can be woven into a fence or more elaborate tunnels and arbors. Just keep tucking in new shoots as they appear.

Site and size

In siting a hedge, remember that you will need access to both sides. On sloping land a hedge will redirect frost, which flows downward like water. To prevent a frost pocket, hedges at the bottom of a slope are better pruned at their base to let the frost through.

The taller the hedge the more shade it will create and the more nutrients and water it will take from plants nearby. If a very tall hedge feels overbearing, take it out and start again with something more suitable. The fast-growing evergreen Leyland cypress (x Cupressocyparis leylandii) is a giant which needs severe pruning from an early age, twice a year, or it soon gets out of control.

Planting

Deciduous varieties are best planted in fall and evergreens in spring, but the ground can be prepared earlier and covered with a weed-suppressing barrier (black plastic, straw, or leaves).

Mark the area to be dug with string. Dig and prepare a trench at least 3 feet (90cm) wide. If taking turf off, cut in 1 foot (30cm) squares and skim underneath the grass (about 2 inches or 5cm) so that it comes up whole. Set this aside because it can be turned over later at the bottom of the trench. Dig a 3 feet (90cm) wide trench in 1 foot (30cm) lines across the 3 feet (90cm) width. Set the first lot of soil aside at the other end of the trench and dig the second section. If there is turf, turn grass side down in the base of the trench or fill with 4 inches (10cm) of well-rotted compost or manure. Put the next excavation of soil on top.

Bare-rooted cuttings (whips) are cheaper than pot-grown plants, although pot-grown plants may be better grown and less prone to drying. Plant 1 1/2–3 feet (50cm–90cm) apart, depending on vigor and bushiness; dwarf varieties 10–12 inches (25–30cm) apart. Apply a top dressing of blood, fish, and bone and mulch to help retain water and suppress weeds. If rabbits and deer are a problem, protect the hedge with chicken wire up to 3 feet (90cm) high, attached to stakes 18 inches (45cm) from the plants to either side.

Pinch out tips of flowering hedges at planting time to encourage bushy growth.

Keep the hedge well watered for the first year. Young hedge plants, especially evergreens, can suffer from the drying effects of wind so they may need a protective windbreak at first.

Cutting

Hedges are best trained from the start. Exceptions are beech and hornbeam —allow these to reach just above the height you want before cutting back. Tapering the sides so the hedge is slightly narrower at the top than the bottom will encourage good thick growth at the base.

Cut hedges in fall to avoid disturbing nests in spring. For vigorous growers or hedges that you want to keep tightly clipped, cut as often as necessary between early summer and late fall. Treat flowering hedges like individual shrubs: cut after flowering if they bloom before midsummer and in early spring if they bloom later.

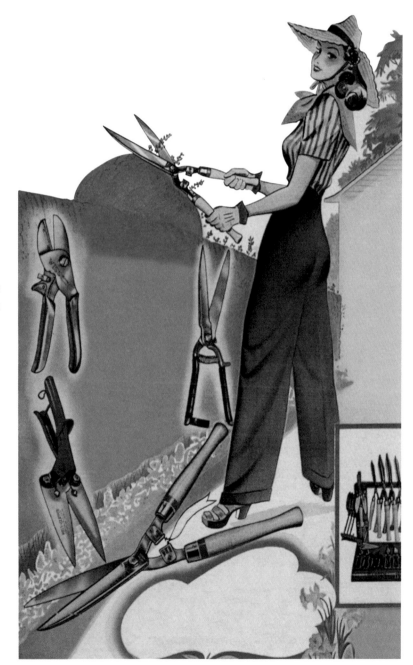

chapter 3 *The Taste*

There is nothing quite like the taste of ripe vegetables fresh from the garden or raspberries plucked straight from the cane. The fresher the food you eat, the better it is for you nutritionally.

If you grow your own food you will know it has not been sprayed with dangerous pesticides, genetically modified, or injected with colorings. Not everyone has the time, space, or desire to grow rows of vegetables or an orchard of fruit. Even so, there is always room for growing one or two things. Sometimes these are already there without your realizing—nasturtiums have a peppery taste and look pretty mixed into salad, as do pansies and the petals of marigolds and daisies.

Growing herbs

Herbs are not highly bred, fussy plants. They have changed little from the original wild species, so understanding a herb's origins is the key to its few requirements.

A great many of our culinary herbs come from around the Mediterranean, thriving in poor, stony soil, being nibbled by passing goats and rabbits. So in the garden they will do best in full sun in a soil that is light and free-draining, while regular trimming, or pinching out shoots to eat will keep them young and fresh. Indeed, too many nutrients in the soil will just result in sappy, tasteless growth.

On heavy soils, incorporate a low-nutrient soil improver, or grit, to improve drainage. Raised beds will help you to control clay soils.

Separate beds will also mean that the fertility of the soil can be adjusted for different plants. Gravel around drought-tolerant plants, like rosemary or lavender, will prevent the base of the plant from becoming waterlogged and will also suppress weeds.

Herbs in pots and containers

Pots are a practical way of growing herbs that looks good too. If space is limited they can be arranged on a special display unit, or shelves against a wall or fence. Gather a collection of culinary herbs in pots near the kitchen.

Use any container with a minimum depth of 12 inches (30cm); it should be large enough and have enough moisture retention in the soil to be able to last two days without watering, except in extremely hot and dry climates. Ensure that it has sufficient drainage holes and put a layer of stones or gravel in the bottom to improve drainage. For herbs that like a lighter soil, add about a handful of gravel to every five handfuls of multi-purpose potting compost. (Sand is another option but can encourage ants.) Add a sprinkling of lime for smaller pots and up to two handfuls for a large pot. Check at least once a day in sunny weather but don't overwater—once spreading plants such as marjoram or thyme cover the soil there will be less surface evaporation.

Drought-tolerant herbs
curry plant (*Helichrysum italicum*)
lavender (*Lavandula* spp.)
rosemary (*Rosmarinus officinalis*)
sage (*Salvia officinalis*)
thyme (*Thymus* spp.)
wormwood (*Artemisia absinthium*)

Herbs for damp or boggy areas
bugle (*Ajuga reptans*)
meadowsweet (*Filipendula ulmaria*)
mint (*Mentha* spp.)
sweet violet (*Viola odorata*)
valerian (*Valeriana officinalis*)
woodruff (*Gallium odoratum*)

Herbs in beds and borders

There is absolutely no need to segregate herbs from other garden plants. Indeed, many herbs, especially aromatic ones like sage, rosemary and lavender, will encourage pollinating insects into the border and help protect other plants. Their varied growing habits mean there is a place for them in all parts of the garden.

Different colored thymes make attractive groundcover and thrive in the sharp drainage of rock gardens. They will also soften the edges of beds and borders and will not mind the lawn mower clipping them accidentally.

The onion family is especially versatile, and they can be as decorative as their non-edible allium relations. Garlic (*Allium sativum*) will not only keep vampires away but will also provide a clump of delicate pale pink or greeny white flowers. New bulbs will form under the leaves ready for digging up and eating. The fresh, grassy leaves of chives (*Allium schoenoprasum*), topped by bobbles of pink flowerheads, will also make an ornamental

clump or fringe, as will white-flowered Chinese chives (*Allium tuberosum*) or the coarser perennial Welsh onions (*Allium fistulosum*) with creamy green-white heads. All the onion family is reputed to deter rabbits—not an infallible method, but it is worth trying.

Tall, feathery fennel (*Foeniculum vulgare*) will give height to a border and comes in both green or with a lovely bronze flush. Dill (*Anethum graveolens* var. *hortorum*) is not so tall but will add a similar airiness, and lovage is a tall, sturdy perennial whose celery-like leaves can grow over 6 feet (2m).

Many herbs lend themselves to being planted in drifts through a border. Hyssop (*Hyssopus officinalis*), a healing herb for colds, is a low-growing evergreen perennial with rich blue flowers in late summer. Purple-flowered summer savory (*Satureja hortensis*) also makes a small bush. Coriander (*Coriandrum sativum*), with its small white flowers and delicious, spicy-tasting seeds, looks like a miniature dill. Lemon balm (*Melissa officinalis*), a Mediterranean perennial with light green leaves and tiny white or pale purple flowers, gives off the scent of lemons all summer. Sorrel (*Rumex acetosa var. hortensis*) is a subtly handsome plant, although a patch may raise a few eyebrows since it looks like its relation, the dock. The raw leaves, sweet yet pungent, taste delicious in salads and make a good sauce or soup.

Some herbs—notably the mints and comfrey —are invasive and need to be restricted. Plant them into a large bucket without a base or a pot that is half-sunk into the ground.

Some popular kitchen herbs

Basil (*Ocimum basilicum*)
Tender annual 12–18in (30–45cm) tall. Short growing season, needs sun and warmth.
Sow in pots in a warm place. Transplant as little as possible, so multi-seeding is a good idea (see page 36). Be consistent in watering and pinch out tops regularly or plants will straggle or bolt. Purple-leaved, crinkly, and small-leaved varieties as well as the familiar shiny green leaves are available.

Bay (*Laurus nobilis*)
This almost hardy evergreen tree can be kept small in a pot and be cut or clipped into a pyramid or other shape.
Choose a sheltered position on rich, well-drained soil, and in cold areas mulch the root area well to protect. Dry the leaves before using to flavor sauces and casseroles.

Chives (*Allium schoenoprasum*)
Perennial, clumps about 12in (30cm) tall. Moist soil; tolerates light shade.
Sow *in situ* in spring or fall or as cells transplanted in a clump. Old clumps should be lifted, divided, and re-planted every three years. Cut regularly during summer. Allow some to develop the edible pink flowers, but remove hardened flower stalks once picked.

Dill (*Anethum graveolens*)
Annual, about 2ft. (60cm) tall. Free-draining, light soil in sun.
The whole plant has a delicate aniseed taste. Use the feathery leaves in salads or with fish, and dry the seeds for flavoring fish dishes and pickles.

Fennel (*Foeniculum vulgare*)
Similar characteristics to dill but much larger and stronger, up to 6ft. (2m) tall. Throw some stems on the barbecue to give the smoke a lovely aroma.

Marjoram (*Origanum vulgare*)
Low-growing perennial up to 16in (40cm) tall. Free-draining, poor to moderately fertile soil in sun.

Sow in spring in rows 8in (20cm) apart and thin or prick out to 10in (25cm) apart. Divide large clumps in fall or spring. A pot filled with marjoram can last for a year. Cut it for flavoring tomatoes, savory dishes or salads. Oregano is a wild form of marjoram.

Parsley (*Petroselinum crispum*)
Biennial 12–18in (30–45cm) tall in two varieties: broad-leaved, hardier and easier to grow; curly-leaved more decorative. Moist, fertile soil.
Sow *in situ* or in cells. Seed is slow to germinate if the soil is cold, so pouring boiling water over the new seeds helps to soften the seed case. Sow in spring and late summer to get all-year round parsley and let some go to seed for continuing the supply. Cut flowering shoots to prolong its useful life.

Rosemary (*Rosmarinus officinalis*)
Hardy to frost-tender evergreen shrub, to 5ft. (150cm) in warm, sheltered position. Plant in free-draining, poor to moderately fertile soil.
Buy small plants or propagate by sowing seed indoors in spring or by rooting cuttings under glass in late summer. Low-growing, spreading varieties like "Seven Seas" are best for pots and containers. Bushes can be lightly clipped in mid-spring while it is better to clip hedges after flowering.

Sage (*Salvia officinalis*)
Broad sub-shrub about 12–24in (30–60cm) tall. Well-drained position, in full sunlight.
Can be grown from seed sown under glass in spring but it is easier to buy a small plant. Cut back lightly in mid to late spring to avoid it getting leggy. Soft, gray-green foliage is strongly aromatic and bitter-tasting but good with fatty food like pork or duck. Sometimes forms spikes of purple flowers. There are also varieties with golden variegated and purple leaves.

A herb garden

In the sixteenth century a garden of "simples" (medicinal herbs) was traditionally laid out in a geometric design—a square, rectangle, or circle, with divisions defined by paths that gave easy access to the herbs for harvesting or cultivating.

Formal hedging Box, rosemary, lavender, and hyssop are good.

Informal hedging Plant alpine strawberries, chives, parsley, thyme, and santolina.

Formal geometric herb garden To take an easy form of division, a square is divided into four. A brick path is laid around the square and along the dissecting halves so that there are four quarters. Each quarter may be divided again into smaller quarters or triangles. But to begin, keep it simple and consider four main divisions of herbs: medicinal, culinary, perfume, and craft.

The medicinal section could include plants which flower in midsummer like Yarrow (*Achillea millefolium*) which was used to staunch bleeding during the first World War. Growing to 2 feet (60cm) high, its feathery blue-green foliage is followed in summer by flat white heads of flowers. It is best placed in its square to surround a central, closely planted group of tall plants like the yellow evening primrose (*Oenothera biennis*). Around the outer edge of the square, put white and yellow chamomile (*Chamaemelum nobile*) flowers, which can be used dried to make a calming tea or added to skin creams or shampoos.

The culinary section for midsummer can be edged by the pink flowers and long thin leaves of chives (*Allium schoenoprasum*) with the middle taken by coriander (*Coriandrum sativum*), an annual herb which has been cultivated for over 3000 years and has fine edible leaves with small white to mauve flowers, as well as spicy seeds. In the center of the culinary square, the strong structural leaf shapes of a tight group of borage (with its tubular blue flowers) will make a feeding area for bees and hoverflies.

In the perfume section, start with the pale pink blooms of the damask rose (*Rosa* x *damascena* "Celsiana") which was brought from Persia by the Knights of the Crusades and is used for making rose oil and rose water for perfumes. It grows to about 5 feet (1.5m) high and could be surrounded by the gray leaves and purple spikes of the perennial lavender (*Lavandula angustifolia*) which can be crushed in the hand or harvested for its relaxing scent. Surround it with a contrasting edging of the soft mid-green leaves of lemon balm (*Melissa officinalis*). Bees will not only be attracted, but the foliage will give an aroma of lemons as you brush past it on the pathway.

The craft section could have a basket weaving willow (*Salix alba* var. *vitellina* "Britzensis") which is coppiced annually to produce bright orange-red stems. Plant honesty (*Lunaria annua*) with its moon-like seed pods for flower arranging. White flowers would harmonize with the red stems of the willow but the deep color of the "Munstead Purple" lavender variety could make a more challenging color scheme. Edge this bed with the strong yellows and oranges of the pot marigold (*Calendula officinalis*). The petals are used as a food dye for dairy products and as a substitute for saffron in rice. They can also be eaten in salads and are used as a soothing skin ointment.

These are suggestions of herb plantings to get your imagination going in order to make your own personal selection of herbs. Make sure that your herbs have similar needs for soil and light requirements, and be aware of the flowering times that will provide your preferred color combinations.

Harvesting and preserving

Herbs can be trimmed and picked throughout the growing season and used immediately. For harvesting larger amounts, wait until perennial plants are established and avoid cutting from a weak plant. Vigorous plants like mint or comfrey can be cut to the ground two or three times in a growing season.

Most leafy herbs reach their potency just before flowering. After this the texture of the leaves hardens. Unless you are growing a herb for its seeds or flowers, or want it to self-seed, remove flowers to encourage the production of new leaves

To harvest for drying, choose a warm but not too sunny day. Collect around mid-morning after the night-time moisture has dissipated but before the sun has evaporated the essential oils. Use sharp secateurs or scissors so that the remaining foliage is not torn. Spread the stems out on newspaper or screens and leave in a cool, airy place indoors to dry. Alternatively, wrap them in newspaper and hang them upside down somewhere cool and dry. They can be dried more quickly in an oven turned to the very lowest heat. When they have dried, spread them on newspapers, strip the stalks, and crush the leaves. Discard any leaves that look damaged or diseased. Store somewhere cool and dark in labeled airtight containers. They will retain their flavor for up to a year.

Another way to preserve the flavor of herbs such as basil, parsley, fennel leaves, and chives is to freeze them. Seal fresh dry herbs, chopped or in sprigs, in small plastic bags, then freeze, and use as required.

Herbal tips

A relaxing bath after a hard day's work: combine one teaspoon each of rosemary, lavender heads, and marjoram with a tablespoon of oatmeal. Place in a large handkerchief and hang under the bath tap while it is running.

For a pot-pourri: mix rose petals, lavender, pine needles, cinnamon sticks, and marigold petals in a bowl for prettiness and perfume. Adapt and experiment according to availability.

In a sachet to scent linen or clothes and deter moths: wormwood (*Artemisia absinthium*), sage, rosemary, or cotton lavender (*Santolina*).

Grow your own
Can your own

A. Legume plot

2 rows broad beans

spinach intercrop

french marigolds

shelling peas

snow peas (mange tout)

sugar snap peas

Swiss chard (ruby and green)

2 rows dwarf french beans

sweet corn planted in blocks

climbing beans

surrounded by early lettuce

Herbs: summer savory, mint sunk in pots

Flowers: marigolds, Johnny-Jump-Up (wild pansy)

B. Brassica plot

rutabaga (swede)

blocks of arugula (rocket), mustard, cress

summer cabbage

winter cabbage

intercrop lettuces

red cabbage and kohl-rabi

turnips and spring cabbage

broccoli, intercrop purslane

radish and chervil

Chinese cabbage and tat soi

Brussel sprouts, intercrop pak choi

Herbs: parsley, sage

Flowers: nasturtiums

Four Year Clockwise Rotation Plan

D. Potato plot

basil

tomatoes

zucchini (courgettes) and summer squash

pumpkins

early potatoes

followed by leeks (Jul/Aug)

2nd early potatoes

main crop potatoes

Herbs: horseradish & nettles sunk in pots and dotted at ends of rows

Flowers: flax and corn poppies

C. Root plot

celery planted in trench

celeriac and fennel

Beets

onion sets

spring onions and garlic chives

carrots early

carrots main

spring onions and chives

shallots

salsify and scorzonera

parsnips

Which direction do I plant in?

Orientate rows north–south to give each row the maximum sunlight. If this is not possible, plant tall crops behind smaller crops. However, squashes and pumpkins can benefit from the shade of sweetcorn until the cobs are picked and then they get the sun they require to ripen.

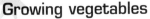

Growing vegetables

The magic of vegetables is in the vitamins and minerals they contain that keep us healthy and alive. Growing your own vegetables gives satisfaction and the security of knowing your very own outdoor larder is storing the tastiest and freshest of food.

Growing vegetables can be quite labor-intensive so it must be fun. Rows of gleaming cauliflowers and ranks of cabbages may look satisfying, but are you going to eat them all? It is true that if a glut of kohlrabi or a surfeit of squash (marrow) is testing your ingenuity as a cook, they can be returned to the soil via the compost pile rather than rotting pungently and uselessly in the garbage, but it is also disheartening. Start by thinking about what you would like to eat and how much time you can devote to growing vegetables. Begin with a small area and work to improve the texture of the soil so that it is easy to cultivate.

Rotation of crops

Vegetables are divided into three main groups:

Brassicas The cabbage family are greedy feeders and require nutrient-rich garden compost or well-rotted manure in the spring. They also like some lime in the soil.

Liking the same conditions are: leeks and the squash family; potatoes, but without the lime (it encourages scab).

Legumes The bean family fix their own nitrogen in the soil and therefore require only a low-nutrient soil improver like leafmold.

Liking the same conditions are: spinach, chard, sweetcorn and lettuce.

Roots High fertility tends to make root crops fork, so these do best following the brassica crop that has been well manured the year before.

Liking the same conditions are: celery and the onion family.

Some vegetables, when grown in the same ground year after year, encourage a build-up of pests and diseases. The problem vegetables include potatoes (nematodes/eelworms); cabbages (clubroot), which includes rutabages (swedes) and turnips; onions (white rot), and carrots (carrot fly). Growing vegetables with similar soil requirements on one plot then moving them away for at least two years will avoid this. There is a set order to rotating crops (see page 89.) For a three-year rotation, join Bed D with Bed B.

Deep beds

Instead of one large vegetable patch, the deep bed method divides the area into self-contained narrow beds—typically three or four—each 3–4 feet (1m or so) wide and as long as you have space for. This makes soil preparation for each crop easier and planting, weeding, watering, and harvesting are all done from paths around the beds. This avoids soil compaction which would mean that micro-organisms work less well and roots would have a harder time extracting nutrients.

With each bed tailored to the needs of a specific range of vegetables, crop rotation is easier and vegetables have the potential to be healthier, bigger, or more productive. Make the paths sufficiently wide for you to walk along and work from easily. The beds' edges can either be the same level as the surrounding paths or built up. Heavier clay soils benefit from raised beds, while free-draining soils dry out if the edges aren't protected. Edging the beds with wood, brick, or tiles protects and separates them from the paths and is particularly suitable for a more formal style kitchen garden.

Over the years the level of topsoil in these beds becomes deeper from successive applications of compost, well-rotted manure, and mulches. With more nutrient-rich earth to root down into, vegetables can be planted closer together, more vegetables can be grown in less space, and there is less room for weeds.

Green manures

These are grown specifically to improve the soil and are dug back in while they are green. They add nutrients, protect the surface when nothing else is growing, and improve soil structure both through their roots and afterward as humus. Many smother weeds and encourage pest predators such as frogs, beetles and hoverflies. Broadcast the seed, rake in lightly, and water with a fine spray. When the crop begins to mature, dig it in, cutting it with a sharp spade as you go, or cut, leave to wilt, and then dig in.

Weeding and watering

Keeping a vegetable garden completely weed-free is a lot of hard work and largely unnecessary. A general commonsense approach is to hoe rows when seedlings are young and then, once the young plants are large enough not to be smothered, spread a good mulch between the rows. The large leaves of vegetables like squash and zucchini (courgettes) will also suppress a lot of weed growth.

Planting by the moon

Old country tradition advises that root crops and spinach and lettuce, which are also close to the ground, be sown or transplanted when the moon is waning. Their roots are strengthened and they are less likely to bolt. Airy and tall plants are best sown or planted as the moon waxes. These are crops like tomatoes, eggplants (aubergines), sweet peppers, beans, and peas. Fruits and vegetables are best eaten fresh while the moon waxes while those that are dried or preserved as jams or sauces are best collected and made while the moon wanes.

Green manures
N = good nitrogen fixer.

Green Manure	Use	Sowing and dig in
Buckwheat (*Fagopyrum esculentum*)	Grows on poor soils, attracts insects, especially hoverflies.	Sow late spring to late summer Dig in after 1–3 months.
Fava beans (Wunter field beans) (*Vicia faba*)	Good for heavy, wet but not waterlogged, soil. Doesn't suppress weeds. N.	Sow fall to early winter Dig in end of winter
Crimson clover (*Trifolium incarnatum*)	Prefers light soils. Attracts insects, especially bees. N.	Sow early spring to late summer. Dig in after 2–3 months; may overwinter from late sowing
Bitter lupin (*Lupinus angustifolius*)	Good for light acid soil but poor weed suppressor. N.	Sow early spring to mid summer (in rows rather than broadcast). Dig in after 2–4 months
Rye (*Secale cereale*)	Good for over-wintering. Good weed suppressant, and improves soil structure.	Sow late summer, early winter: Dig in over winter. Leave a few weeks before sowing a small seed crop as the rye inhibits germination.
Phacelia (*Phacelia tanacetifolia*)	Tolerates most soils; attract bees and hoverflies.	Sow early spring to late summer. Can survive a warm winter if plants are small. Dig in after 1–3 months.
Common vetch (Winter tares) (*Vicia sativa*)	Overwinters from late sowings. Doesn't like acid or dry soils. N.	Sow spring or end of summer (rows rather than broadcast) Dig in after 2–3 months or overwinter.

Mulches and even a covering of weeds, if it is not too dense, will help keep the soil moist, but young plants will still need watering (see page 23–26 for advice on when and how to water most effectively). The critical periods for watering vary from crop to crop (see Vegetable Tables, pages 96–101).

Protecting
Crops will require protection from cold in early spring and pests during the growing season. There are various ways of doing this, from physical barriers to growing strategic plants.

Floating row cover (Horticultural fleece) This light weight covering can be laid over young crops without squashing them and will give protection unless the frost is very severe. It is permeable and will also give protection from birds, bugs (but not slugs and snails) and, provided they don't burrow underneath, small mammals. Put rocks on the edges, giving enough room for the cover to billow upward as seedlings grow. It will cut down on air circulation, so remove once crops are strong enough. It will work equally well over half-hardy bedding plants and strawberries in flower.

Black fly on my beans

Both French and African marigolds discourage black fly on beans and whitefly on greenhouse tomatoes. Their smell is a deterrent while excretions from their roots put off soil nematodes which attack potatoes, strawberries, roses, and some bulbs.

Cloches Tunnel cloches, whether glass or plastic, give good protection. Glass retains heat better and, provided it is clean, will allow more light through. Plastic, either corrugated PVC or soft polyethylene supported by hoops, is lighter, less fragile and much cheaper to buy, but will discolor and become brittle in time. All tunnel cloches will need end covers to retain heat and keep out pests. Hoops can also be used to support floating row covers (horticultural fleece).

Traditional bell cloches are useful for individual tender plants. Clear plastic drink bottles with the base cut off make effective mini-cloches, and the screw top can be taken off for watering or to release trapped heat.

All cloches are difficult to water under and heat soon builds up, so check there is sufficient ventilation and in bright sunshine improvize some form of shade.

Cloches have uses all year round. Placed over the ground two weeks before sowing,

they will warm up the ground for earlier planting. They can be used to harden off plants that have grown under glass and in warm climates, will keep hardy salads cropping over winter. Plants that began life under cloches will be soft and sappy, so introduce them to outside conditions in stages.

Block planting and mini-veg

Growing vegetables closer together than usually advised will give smaller vegetables, which can be more suitable for a small garden. Plant six or seven plants in a 1 foot (30cm) square and you can harvest early and have other seedlings, grown on in cells, ready to plant in their place. Planting closer together will result in mini-veg: sweetcorn, beets, carrots, leeks, and parsnips are all suitable.

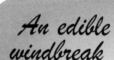

An edible windbreak

For a windbreak with a difference, plant a row or two of Jerusalem artichokes. Looking like extra-tall sunflowers, they will quickly form a slender but effective filter for wind and will develop a good crop of edible tubers even on poor soils.

Maximize your growing season

These are all methods for making the most of the growing season and maximizing land use. It also keeps the ground covered and so suppresses weeds. Basically it is a matter of matching crops and suitable techniques.

Intercrops are fast-growing vegetables grown between or under slower-growing crops, harvested before the main crop grows to maturity. Plant salad leaves, spinach, and spring onions between slower-growing brassicas, leeks, or celeriac. Radishes, ready four weeks after sowing, can mark slower germinating seeds like parsley and parsnip and can also be sown between root crops like scorzonera and salsify. Mustard and cress, usually grown on a windowsill, make a useful marker crop as they are ready in 7–10 days.

Undercrops are the opposite, coming up after the main crop has been harvested. Spreading vegetables like zucchini (courgettes) and pumpkins can be sown under sweetcorn, which will be harvested before the undercrop matures. Carrot and leek seed can be mixed together in a proportion of 3:2 and broadcast. The carrots are harvested first and the leeks follow in fall.

Successional sowing aims for a continuous supply rather than a glut. Sow little and often, every two to three weeks for several months. Sow lettuces and radishes successionally, as well as carrots, oriental greens (calabrese), kohl-rabi, machê (corn salad), arugula (rocket), spinach, spring onions, and turnips.

Many leafy vegetables will grow back if they are cut rather than pulled. "Cut and come again" crops include machê (corn salad), cress, chicory, endive, mustard, many lettuces, orach, purslane and arugula (rocket). A number of seed mixes are sold with this type of harvesting in mind. Sow in blocks and enjoy two to three harvests.

Plot A: the legume plot

Variety	Cultivation	Spacing
Fava beans (Broad beans)	Sow outdoors mid-fall–early winter, or in spring.	2in (5cm) deep, 10in (25cm) apart, 2ft. (60cm) between double rows.
Green beans (French beans)	Sow outdoors early–late spring (protect early sowings). Transplant late spring.	2in (5cm) deep, 10in (25cm) apart, 1ft. (30cm) between rows.
Pole beans (Runner beans)	Sow in small pots late spring or *in situ* late spring–mid summer. Before planting, erect framework of stakes.	2in (5cm) deep, 6–12in (15–30cm) apart in double rows 12–16in (30–40cm) apart, or plant 2 per h at base of stakes; thin to 1.
Shell peas, snow peas (mange tout), sugar snaps	There are early, second early, main crop, and late varieties. Sow successively early spring–mid summer (protect early sowings).	1–2in (3–5cm) deep, 4in (10cm) apart. 1ft. (30c between rows, or double rows 9in (23cm) apart, 18in (45cm) between double rows.

Liking the same conditions

Lettuces–many varieties, bibb, romaine, Boston, looseleaf	Sow every two weeks indoors or in coldframe early spring–high summer; late sowings in situ. Weed between plants until leaves spread to cover ground. Keep moist especially near harvest time or they bolt.	½in (1cm) deep in rows 1ft. (30cm) apart. Thin 6–12in (15–30cm) apart according to variety. Plants transplanted a hand's stretch apart will soc fill space.
Spinach, Swiss chard	Sow late winter/early spring, then leave every 10 days to mid-summer.	1in (2cm) deep, in rows 9in (23cm) apart. Thin plants gradually to 6in (15cm) apart.
Sweet corn	Sow indoors in spring (min. 50ºF/10ºC). Harden off and transplant late spring. Protect with floating row cover (horticultural fleece) until weather improves.	In blocks 12in (30cm) apart each way.

Plot B: the brassica plot

Variety	Cultivation	Spacing
Broccoli	Sow successionally in situ spring–mid summer. Mulch or foliar feed after cutting main head to encourage side growth.	3 seeds per hill, 9in (23cm) apart, in rows 1ft. (30cm) apart. Thin to 1 per hill.
Brussels sprouts	Sow in spring in seedbed, thinly in drills. Thin to 6in (15cm) apart. Transplant late spring/early summer when 3in (8cm) high. Cut leaves half-way down after planting out to limit water loss.	18in (45cm) apart in rows 30in (75cm) apart.
Cabbage—spring	In warm climates, sow in seedbed in late summer. Transplant to growing position in fall. In zones 2–7, start seeds inside and plant out in early spring.	12in (30cm) apart in rows 18in (45cm) apart.
Cabbage—summer, red	Sow in coldframe or seedbed in early spring; transplant in late spring.	18in (45cm) apart in rows 18in (45cm) apart.

Harvest	Notes	All legumes
Late spring–late summer. Pick pods often, when young and tender.	Support with canes and string. Pinch out tops when in flower to swell pods.	After harvest, cut off all legumes at base and dig roots in to return nitrogen to soil.
Summer through to fall. Pick when young green and continuously.	Also climbing varieties.	
Mid-summer–mid fall. Seeds can be dried for winter use.	Tips can be pinched out when plants reach top of support, or stop growth early to make early-cropping dwarf plants.	
Mid-summer–mid fall.	Provide twiggy sticks or net trellises for tendrils to attach to. Where mice are a nuisance set traps or soak seeds in paraffin before sowing.	

Cut when large enough. With looseleaf or young lettuces, harvest leaves as required.	Sunny position for early and late crops, summer ones better in partial shade. Grow as intercrop in any bed with well–fertilized soil. Use thinnings in salads. The stem can sprout again if left but otherwise lift roots for composting.	
Early summer–fall. Pick leaves when reasonable size without disturbing roots. Don't pick more than half the plant.	Early sowing in sunny site, late in shady spot, so plants don't bolt.	
Late summer–mid fall. Test ears (cobs) for tenderness by pulling back outer casing; when ready twist ear off.	Needs sunny sheltered spot in cold areas; not good in cold or wet. Wind-pollinated, so needs to be grown in blocks.	

Harvest	Notes	All brassicas
Summer–fall. After the main tight green head is cut, side shoots sprout smaller heads. Cut these before they flower.		Water needed most at harvest time to prevent bolting. Plant tomatoes or herbs nearby to deter cabbage white butterfly. To protect from cabbage root fly: make each plant a flat collar from carpet or cardboard.
Mid fall–early spring. Harvest sprouts from the bottom of the stem upward.	Long growing season. Sprouts taste best after a frost.	
The following spring. After cutting, make a cross-cut on the stalk and more small cabbages will sprout.	Protect from cabbage root fly maggots with floating row cover (horticultural fleece) .	
High summer–mid fall.		

Plot B: the brassica plot continued

Variety	Cultivation	Spacing
Cabbage—winter	Sow in coldframe or seedbed in late spring. Transplant in summer, when ground is cleared of other crops.	18in (45cm) apart in rows 18in (45cm) apart.
Chinese cabbage, pak choi	Hill sow in situ or successionally in cells through summer. Harden off before transplanting 5 weeks after sowing. Give late transplants protection.	12in (30cm) apart in rows 18in (45cm) apart (pak choi can be closer).
Chop suey greens (shungiku, mizuna)	Very fine seed. Sow successionally from early spring (with protection for early sowings).	Thinly in shallow drills in rows 1ft. (30cm) apart. Thin to 4in (10cm) apart.
Rutabaga (Swede)	Sow direct into rich soil in later spring (early summer in colder areas).	4in (10cm) apart in rows 16–18 in (40–50cm) apart. Thin to about 10in (25cm) as roots grow.
Turnips	Sow quick cultivars successionally early spring–late summer; main crops latter half of summer.	Thinly in drills 1in (2cm) deep or stations 4in (10cm) apart in rows 9in (23cm) apart (main crop 12in (30cm) apart. Thin quick cultivars to 4in (10cm), main crop to 6in (15cm).

Liking the same conditions

Variety	Cultivation	Spacing
Purslane	Sow direct in late spring/early summer or in cell packs in mid-spring to plant out after risk of frost has passed.	In drills 1in (2cm) deep in rows 6in (15cm) apart. Thin to 6in (15cm) apart.
Radish	Sow successionally throughout spring and summer (protect early sowings).	Thinly in drills ½in (1cm) deep in rows 4–6in (10–15cm) apart. Thin to 1in (2cm) apart.
Rocket (Arugula)	Sow outdoors in light soil, early spring–early fall. Summer sowings best in partial shade.	Broadcast in blocks or intercrop.

Plot C: roots, onions and celery

Variety	Cultivation	Spacing
Beets	In cells in early spring, 2 seeds thinned to 1. Transplant when 4 true leaves show. Or sow successionally in situ mid-spring–mid-summer. Protect with row cover (fleece) when cold to prevent bolting. Water often in hot, dry weather to keep roots crisp.	In drills ½in (1cm) deep in rows 6–12in (15–30cm) apart. Thin to 1–3in (2–8cm) apart, according to size of root required.
Carrots: early and main crop	Long-rooted varieties need deep soil while shorter ones will grow in shallow or heavy soils. Sow successionally: early crop early spring–late summer; main crop mid-spring–early summer.	In drills ½in (1cm) deep in rows 6in (15cm) apart. Thin to 2in (5cm) apart, a little wider spaced for main crops.
Celery	Sow in cells, in gentle heat, in early spring. Thin to 2–3 seedlings. Harden off and transplant outdoors beginning of summer, with protection at first.	In blocks 6–12in (15–30cm) apart. Closer planting produces more slender stems.

Harvest	Notes	All brassicas
Late fall–early spring.	Do not overfeed overwintering cabbages—lush leaves will be damaged by frost.	
Late summer–mid winter. Stumps can sprout new leaves after cutting.		
4–5 weeks after sowing, when 4in (10cm) high. Pull whole, or cut individual leaves as needed. Remove flower buds to encourage tender leaves.	Tend to run to seed in dry hot weather. Can also be sown in early fall for winter crop. Young leaves can be eaten raw in salads while older ones are better steamed lightly.	
Approximately 20–30 weeks after sowing. Best lifted by early winter as they become woody.	Purple skinned have best flavor.	
Harvest after 5 weeks from early sowings, 10 weeks for main crop. Pull early turnips at 2in (5cm) diameter and main crop at 3in (7–8cm).	Late turnips can be kept in ground till midwinter; any still growing in following spring can be used as early greens.	

Harvest	Notes	
5–8 weeks from sowing. Cut at 2in (5cm) high for cut-and-come-again seedling crops, or pick regularly as required.	Good intercrop. When plants run to seed at end of cutting season, cut plants to ground and they may resprout.	
20–30 days after sowing, when radishes show above the soil.	Good intercrop and in shade of other plants in mid summer.	
About 3 weeks from sowing, when 2in (5cm) high. They will grow again and can be cut 2–3 more times.		

Harvest	Notes
7–13 weeks after sowing, when roots are the right size. If left too long, roots become woody.	Easy to grow. Globe cultivars will grow in containers. Always twist foliage to remove, rather than cut, to avoid bleeding.
Pull early sowings by hand as soon as they are large enough to eat. Main crop ready mid-fall; ease out with a fork. Remove soil, and twist foliage off. Select firm, whole carrots to store in boxes of sand.	To protect against carrot fly, surround with polyethylene barrier 15in (38cm) high, or plant onions alongside (flies are attracted by smell). Do not leave thinnings close by and thin in the evening when carrot flies are less active.
Latter part of summer–early fall.	Self-blanching celery easier than trench. Stems are paler if grown in a block; surround blocks with straw to blanch outer plants further.

Plot C: roots, onions, and celery continued

Variety	Cultivation	Spacing
Garlic and shallots	Plant as soon as weather allows at end of winter. Weed carefully and protect from birds pulling up tips. In mid-summer remove soil from bulb clumps to help ripening.	Plant garlic cloves 1in (2cm) deep, 4in (10cm) apart, in rows 6–8in (15–20cm) apart. Press shallots into ground 6in (15cm) apart so tips just show.
Onions	Frost-tolerant, sun to partial shade. Plant sets (small bulbs) early spring, when soil is workable. Push into soil with pointed tip just showing. Protect from cold and birds.	2–4in (5–10cm) apart in rows 10–12in (25–30cm) apart, according to bulb size required.
Spring onions	Sow successively at 3-week intervals early spring–early summer. Grow close together to prevent bulbs growing too large.	In drills ½in (1cm) deep in rows 4in (10cm) apart or in bands 3in (8cm) wide, 9in (23cm) between bands. Thin by harvesting to ½–1in (1–2cm) apart.
Parsnips	Sow successively late winter–late spring. Slow to germinate. Water and hoe regularly through summer.	Thinly in shallow drills, or 2–3 seeds stations 6in (15cm) apart, in rows 8in (20cm) apart. Thin to strongest seedling 6in (15cm) apart.
Salsify, scorzonera	Soil should be stone-free if possible to help roots grow unimpeded. Sow direct in mid–late spring. Remove weeds by hand to avoid damaging roots. Keep moist and mulch after final thinning.	2–3in (5–7.5cm) deep, in stations 6in (15cm) apart, rows 1ft (30cm) apart. Thin to plant per station.

Plot D: potatoes, leeks, and the squash family

Variety	Cultivation	Spacing
Potatoes; early, second earlies and main crop	Prepare ground with annual dressing of well-rotted garden compost or manure; do not lime as this encourages potato scab. In late winter "chit" seed potatoes: place with as many eyes as possible upward and cover with newspaper. Put in a light, warm place. When shoots are about 1in (2cm) long move to cooler position. Plant out earlies in early spring, 2nd earlies 2 weeks later and main crop 2 weeks after that. Delay if soil is cold and wet.	In trenches or holes 3–6in (8–15cm) deep. Earlies 12in (30cm) apart, 18in (45cm) between rows. 2nd earlies and main crop: 18in (45cm) apart, 2½ (60cm) between rows. Cover with 2in (5cm) of soil. As sprouts grow above the soil, hill soil up about them.
Leeks	Fertile soil, moisture-retentive but not waterlogged in winter. A good crop to follow potatoes which loosen the earth. Sow in seedbed early–late spring 1in (2cm) deep, thin to 1in (2cm) apart in rows 6in (15cm) apart. Transplant when space available in summer. Water seedbed well before digging up transplants.	Use a dibble (dibber) to make holes 6in (15cm) deep and 6–8 in (15–20cm) apart, rows 1ft (30cm) apart. Drop transplants into holes and water in but do not fill holes with soil – the leeks will swell to fill them.
Squashes (summer and winter) and pumpkins	Fertile soil in well-drained, warm sunny position. Sow indoors, 2–3 seeds per small pot. Press oval seeds on sides just below surface of compost. Prick out and pot on before hardening off. Plant out mid- to early summer. Or sow 2–3 seeds in situ in late spring; thin to 1. Water only until established. Extra feeding will produce more leaves, and may be needed as fruits are formed.	Bush cultivars: 2–3ft. (60–90cm) apart in rows 3–4ft. (1–1.2m) apart. Trailing: 4–6ft. (1.2–1.8m) apart in rows 6ft. (1.8m) apart.

Harvest	Notes
Late summer as stems and leaves begin to yellow and bend. Loosen bulbs gently and leave to dry on surface. If wet, spread out under cover.	Separate clumps of shallots to help dry. Store well-dried bulbs in string bags in cool but frost-free place.
When foliage turns yellow and tops bend over naturally, pull bulbs gently. Leave tops to die down and outer skin becomes paper dry, about 10 days. If it's wet, take inside and lay in airy boxes or on trays.	Sets are easier to grow, but more varieties available as seed. If onion fly is prevalent, grow under fine nets or fleece. Water well in early stages but not later; overwatering will damage crop. Dry stems can be plaited and bulbs hung for storage.
As required, using thinnings. Ready 8 weeks after sowing.	
Late fall onward, when foliage begins to die down. Lift as needed with fork. To store: leave in ground and lift when needed. Clear ground by spring for next crop.	Always use fresh seed. Because of slow germination, mix seed. Leave some roots to flower in second year—the large flower spike will attract beneficial insects.
Leave roots in ground in fall and winter, dig up as required.	Tops of both can be blanched to be eaten in salads in spring. Cut back leaves to 1in (2cm) and earth up to a depth of 6in (15cm) over the tops. Scrape soil away in spring and cut shoots when about 6in (15cm) long.

Harvest	Notes
3 months after planting. Earlies: high summer; 2nd earlies: late summer; main crop: from early fall. Dig up as foliage dies down and dig out all tubers to avoid disease and regrowth.	Choose certified small seed potatoes. Hilling up controls weeds and keeps tubers covered so they don't go green. Can be mulched with grass mowings, hay or straw. Potatoes can also be grown on soil surface under a mulch. Top up the mulch as they grow. Flowering shows tubers are large enough but not all varieties flower. To store, knock off soil and store healthy potatoes in burlap or paper sacks to avoid sweating.
Early fall–late spring. Lift as required.	Varieties include taller, slimmer, earlier or later types. Alternative site is to follow beans: they benefit from nitrogen fixed by beans but add a medium-fertility soil improver. If soil is too rich, growth becomes sappy and less frost hardy. Can be planted as an intercrop. Their strong root structure is good for soil structure.
Summer squash and zucchini (courgettes): cut when 4–6in (10–15cm) long; keep picking when small to continue supply. Others: twist to break off when ready. Well-ripened winter squash and pumpkins will store for 6–12 months in an airy place.	Choose bush cultivars for limited space. Trailing cultivars can climb or sprawl under taller crops; can be stopped when side stems reach 2ft (60cm). To maintain good drainage, mound the soil up before planting on top. An empty plant pot inserted into the soil will help water reach the roots. Male flowers can be eaten after pollination or to lessen the number of fruits per plant. Mulch with straw to keep fruit clean. Put a board under large fruit.

Tomatoes, sweet peppers, chilies, and eggplants (aubergines)

These tender fruiting bushes all need similar care. Peppers and chilies are available in increasing variety and color (green peppers are just unripe red ones). Eggplants (aubergines), too, come in several shapes and sizes, including small white ovoids, which explains their alternative name of eggplant. But it is tomatoes that offer the greatest range: for indoors, for outdoors; as bushes or staking types; from cherry size to great round "beefsteak" varieties; red, yellow, and even striped. Choose a variety that suits your taste and the conditions you can provide.

Sow seed inside in gentle heat in pots or trays. Prick out into 3 inch (7cm) pots and pot on again if they become too large before it is warm enough to plant out. Plants destined for a greenhouse can be potted on into larger pots or growbags or moved into a prepared bed as soon as they are sturdy enough. They like a fertile soil, slightly acid and well-drained. Harden off outdoor plants gradually and transplant to their final homes when all danger of frost has passed. They will need a warm, sheltered, sunny spot, and may be happier in large pots or grow bags than in the open ground.

Staked tomatoes will need tying to stakes. To prevent their branching, pinch out suckers with your fingers while they are still small.

Overwatering or overfeeding reduces crop flavor but keep containers moist and plants watered in dry weather when fruit is forming. Tomatoes and eggplants (aubergines), in particular, will need regular liquid fertilising once the fruit start to appear.

Don't let the frost get your unripe tomatoes

If you are left with unripe outdoor tomatoes as the first frosts arrive, pull up the plants and hang upside down in a frost-free place to finish ripening. Or pick healthy green fruit and put in a cool place—placing one red tomato among green ones is said to help them ripen.

Asparagus

An established asparagus bed will crop for up to 20 years, producing edible shoots for about six weeks in late spring.

The priority is good drainage. Once the bed is weed-free, dig in well-rotted garden compost or manure in fall and leave over the winter before forking and raking. Asparagus can be grown from seed, but that means an extra year before you can enjoy it. Buy one-year-old crowns (easier to transplant than older crowns) and protect them from drying out before planting.

Planting asparagus

Dig a trench 12 inches (31cm) wide and 8 inches (20cm) deep. Space a second trench 4.5 feet (1.5m) away. Mix grit into soil if necessary to give good drainage. Put this soil in the bottom of the trench in a rounded ridge, 3 inches (8cm) high. Stand the asparagus crowns on the ridge with their roots spread out and spaced 18 inches (46cm) apart. Do not fill to the top of the trench with soil but lightly cover the crowns until the roots do not show. Fill the rest of the trench in during the season as growth develops, keeping the crowns covered and encouraging the roots to grow deeply.

In early spring apply a dressing of well-rotted compost or manure, gently so as to not disturb the shoots. Asparagus also appreciates a seaweed mulch.

Cut no shoots the first year and only one thick stem from each plant the next year. In the third year cut all the stems but stop after five weeks. After that, harvest all stems when 3–4 inches (8–10cm) above ground, cutting with a knife as low as possible below soil level.

Globe artichoke

Grown for its partially edible flowerbuds. These attractive plants, with their silvery foliage, are best grown from shoots taken from mature plants. Cut or buy in mid-spring and plant 3 feet (90cm) apart in fertile soil. Give them a sunny, sheltered position in warm climates and keep well watered until established.

Harvest the flowerheads before the scales start to open, from late summer in the first year, a little earlier in subsequent years. In late fall, cut down old stems and cover with straw. In spring apply a top dressing of well-rotted garden compost or manure. Plants are usually renewed after three years as the heads become smaller.

Rhubarb

Despite being eaten like fruit, rhubarb is actually a vegetable. Plant in the fall, 3 feet (90cm) between plants, in fairly acid soil with plenty of well-rotted manure. Do not pull the stalks for the first year, leaving the goodness to go back into the plant.

To "force" rhubarb, cover plants in January with thick layers of straw or a large open ended bucket, barrel, or chimney pot which you can wrap with straw, bubblewrap, or cardboard to insulate and encourage growth. The long red stalks will steadily grow up through the dark of its covering to be pulled, ready to eat in spring.

Growing soft fruit

The joys of fresh berries are hard to miss. Soft fruit are not difficult to cultivate and bushes can often be planted among shrubs and in flower beds. Currants and gooseberries are a good choice if space is limited, because they are self-pollinating and one bush will set an adequate crop on its own. They can even be grown in large pots.

If you are planning on a more ambitious scale, plant soft fruit bushes around your vegetable patch or in a bed of their own, which will make them easier to look after.

Strawberries

The main strawberry crop is in early summer, but early cultivars start fruiting in late spring and the late cultivars (perpetuals) continue fruiting into the fall. Twelve plants is the minimum required to provide a good harvest. Strawberries need to be moved every fourth year to avoid a build-up of disease; ideally they should also not return to the same place for six years.

Strawberries are not fussy but grow best in a slightly acidic, sandy loam with good humus. Choose an open site in full sun, because they require winter cold to start the flowering process and summer sun to ripen. Weed and dig the bed in summer, incorporating well-rotted manure or fertile garden compost. High fertility will produce leaves rather than fruit, so this will be sufficient for the three-year life of the bed. More important than fertility is good drainage—on heavy land, grow strawberries in raised beds.

Strawberries reproduce themselves by throwing out long stems at the end of which a new plant develops. These are called runners. They are best planted in late summer, although pot-grown plants can be planted at any time, even in late spring just before they are due to fruit. Space 12 inches (30cm) apart in staggered rows 18 inches (45cm) apart, spreading the roots out and firming in well.

Keeping off predators

Many wild animals love soft fruit. An animal-proof fence should ban foxes, rabbits, and deer, but only a fruit cage or netting will keep off squirrels and birds. Netting some fruit can be an awkward, prickly business. Whirring wires, strings with rattling bottle tops, or a fake bird of prey will all deter birds for a short time. The trick with bird-scarers is to keep changing them before the birds become used to them.

Keep away birds!

Paint small strawberry-sized stones red and scatter them among the strawberry plants. These give birds a nasty shock and they don't try to eat your strawberries again.

Water regularly to help swell the fruit, preferably in the morning so that leaves and fruit are dry by nightfall. This helps prevent fungal disease from developing on damp foliage and also deters slugs. As the small fruit begin to show, mulch with straw to keep them clean and dry and to conserve moisture.

As soon as picking is finished, cut off the old leaves, leaving the crowns and young leaves untouched. Collect the old dry mulch to get rid of pests and diseases. Fork in a light sprinkling of potash fertilizer around the plants, a handful per yard or meter, and water thoroughly if the ground is dry.

Let runners root themselves across the bed to form an increasingly thick, weed-suppressing mat. Runners from your own plants can be used to make a new bed, but if in doubt about their health, buy new ones.

Alpine strawberries

These are just like miniature versions of their full-size cousins, with flavor-packed fruits no bigger than a thumbnail. You will need at least 30 plants to get a decent amount of fruit, but they spread quickly and do not need moving every few years. They also make an interesting edging to a flower border.

Strawberry pots

These are an attractive idea, especially if you do not need a huge crop. The plants grow through holes in the sides as well as out of the top, producing a cascade of fruit and leaves, and the pot can be turned to get maximum sun. To help water reach the bottom of a tall container, put a plastic pipe 2–3 inches (5–7cm) in diameter down the center and fill with gravel. Fill the pot with potting soil gradually, planting as you go, rather than trying to force young plant roots in through the holes afterward.

Raspberries

Raspberries grow on long upright canes 6 feet (2m) or more tall and should give a good crop for up to 12 years. You can extend the cropping period by planting both summer- and fall-fruiting varieties.

Raspberries like a slightly acid soil rich in organic matter with good drainage. Prepare the ground a month before planting by digging a trench and add a bucketful of compost or well-rotted manure for every yard or meter. Backfill the trench and sprinkle a slow-release fertilizer like bonemeal over the surface.

Plant bare-rooted canes in late fall or, if this is not possible, in early spring. Space 18 inches (45cm) apart with 6 feet (1.8m) between rows. Cut back the cane to a bud 1 inch (2–3cm) above the soil and then, when new growth shows in spring, cut this old cane down to ground level. Container-grown plants can be planted at any time and the main canes do not need cutting back.

It is best to not pick fruit in the first year, and on container-grown canes, rub out the flowers to prevent fruit forming.

Cane supports

There are many systems of support. String, wire or mesh can be stretched between poles and the new canes tied to it. A single 6 feet (2m) post can be planted with 2 raspberries at the base and as much as 12 canes grown up it, tied around with string at one-third and two-thirds of the way up. There are both single and double post and wire systems. The single system is the easiest to look after and allows

individual canes to be tied in, while spacing allows for light and air.

A post and wire support system is built with strong end-posts with angled struts and other uprights at 10 feet (3.3m) intervals. The posts are 3 inches x 3 inches (90cm x 90cm) and buried 2 feet (61cm) in the ground with 6 feet (2m) above. Three rows of plain galvanized fence wire are strung with bolts through the endposts and attached with galvanized wire staples to the posts in between, at 2.5 feet (76cm), 3.5 feet (1.3m) and 5.5 feet (1.8m) from the ground.

When they get to the top wire, tie in and wind the tips of the cane around it to give more stability in strong winds.

Summer raspberries fruit on canes that grew the year before. After fruiting, cut these old canes down to the ground without leaving a stub to collect pests or diseases. The new canes will already be growing well. Thin out any weak ones or those growing outside the limit of the row, to leave about 10 or 12 per yard or meter. Tie them in to their supports and mulch with compost.

Fall-fruiting raspberries can either be tied to supports or left free-standing. Do not thin the canes, but leave them loosely tied after harvest. In late winter cut them down to the ground and mulch well. In early spring apply a general fertilizer followed by a mulch of hay or straw.

You can increase or renew your stock from the rooted suckers that raspberries produce. Just cut the sucker away from the parent root and replant immediately where you want it.

Blackberries and hybrid berries

Boysenberries, loganberries, tayberries, and others are all varying hybrids between raspberries and blackberries. Like cultivated blackberries, they are vigorous growers and some can be thorny. They like similar conditions as raspberries do but allow 6–15 feet (2–5m) between plants, according to their vigor. One good plant is often enough.

Like raspberries they need some support, but you will probably need 8 feet (2.5m) posts to allow for the extra-long stems. Alternatively, grow them up a wall or sturdy fence, tied into wires threaded through vine eyes.

Tying hybrid berries

In the second and subsequent years, the new growth is tied to the top wire to keep it separate from last year's canes, which will be harvested in the current year. After these have fruited, cut them to the ground, untie the new canes from the top wire, and tie them where the old canes were. For instance, tie 3 or 4 canes to each wire except the top one, going in alternate directions. Leave the center free for the current year's growth to grow up and be attached to the top wire. When the canes have fruited and been cut down, take the new growths from the center and tie them to each side on the bottom 3 wires.

Black currants

Juicy and richly flavored, black currants make great pies and preserves as well as being good eaten fresh. They also have a high vitamin C content. They are hardy and reliable, although late frost can damage flowers. They are unfussy about soil type, but will need fertile conditions if they are pruned hard.

Black currants grow into quite broad bushes and a single bush can be sufficient in a small garden. Buy 2-year-old plants, certified to be disease-free and plant between fall and early spring. Incorporate well-rotted garden compost and a scattering of bonemeal into the soil and plant deeply, 1–2 inches (3–5cm) below the old soil mark. Space bushes 4 feet (1.2m) apart, 6 feet (1.8m) for more vigorous varieties. Water well and apply a thick mulch of well-rotted bulky organic compost or manure. Cut all branches back to one or two buds above soil level.

Start pruning in the second year after planting. The dangling strands (called strigs) of berries are borne mainly on one-year-old wood, which means that new stems are required each year. Between late fall and early spring each year, remove up to one-third of the old wood to encourage new growth from beneath the soil.

In summer it can be helpful to take off diseased leaves from the tips and some more leaves to let the sun on to the fruit—but beware that this also makes the fruit more visible to birds.

The worst disease of black currants is bud mite, when buds become round and swollen. Remove and destroy, as an infestation may lead to a reversion virus. You will need expert advice to identify the disease but, if confirmed, the plants will need to be destroyed. This is why it is important to buy certified plants.

Red currants and white currants

Soil requirements and preparation are similar to black currants, but these will tolerate partial shade and will even produce fruit when grown on a north-facing wall or fence. Plant between fall and spring when conditions are suitable, but preferably in fall to give time for the roots to establish themselves. Space bushes 5 feet (1.5m) apart and work in some well-rotted compost. Do not manure, otherwise the bushes will grow too vigorously and winds may break the branches.

After planting, cut all branches back by half to an outward-facing bud. Shorten sideshoots to two or three buds. Repeat this process in subsequent years.

The clusters of fruit grow on short spurs produced from old wood and at the base of sideshoots formed the previous year. Bushes are usually grown as an open-centered goblet shape on a short stem. Keep 8–10 main branches to maintain this shape and remove any shoots growing inward.

In summer identify the leading shoot of a branch and don't prune it. Cut all sideshoots back to five leaves. This removes pest colonies and sappy growth and also improves air circulation, helping the sun to get to the fruit and ripen it.

Gooseberries

Gooseberries will grow with little direct sunlight but the fruit is improved if they receive sun for at least half the day. When siting, feeding, and mulching, treat them much the same as red currants.

Pruning is also similar to red currants, but leave the sideshoots longer to allow more fruit to grow. Gooseberries react vigorously to pruning, turning into spiky skewers if the leaders are cut. Prune sensibly so that you can harvest the fruit by getting your hand inside the bush without catching on the thorns. The larger fruit borne by pruned bushes will be well worth it. Gooseberries also have a habit of throwing up shoots from the base. Cut these away, as well as any less than 1 foot (30cm) above the ground which will droop to ground level once heavy with fruit.

Blueberries

The blueberry, related to the cranberry, has a subtle sheen like suede. Eat it fresh or in pies. Some cultivars crop reasonably alone but two or three different types will cross-pollinate and produce more berries. Fruiting will start in the second summer after planting and with maturity one bush can give a crop of 6 lb (3kg) of fruit. Bushes grow to a height and spread of about 5 feet (1.5m) and their fall color makes them an attraction among ornamental shrubs.

Blueberries require an acid soil (pH5.5 or below) and damp but not waterlogged soil. If you don't have the right conditions you can grow a bush in a large pot. Use acidic (ericaceous) compost and water with rainwater.

Buy two- or three-year-old plants and plant in fall or early spring. Mulch with composted bark or pine needles. Fruit is borne on two- and three-year-old branches, so in winter cut out some of the stems which have already borne fruit to encourage new growth. If birds are a problem, net the bush while the fruit blueberries are ripening. Harvest when the berries come away easily, and have been blue for a week.

TREES THAT THRIVE

Growing fruit trees

An orchard is a magical space at any time of year: in spring when blossoms open and bees hum, in summer as glossy cherries and succulent plums ripen, in fall when a treasury of rosy apples and golden pears appears, and in winter when all is quiet and the leafless, gnarled branches gather their strength.

People hesitate to grow fruit trees for two reasons: they feel they haven't the space or they think the pruning and maintenance will be too complicated and time-consuming. But neither need be the case.

The introduction of trees grown on dwarfing rootstock means fruit trees can grow in the mixed border or on a patch of lawn. Dwarf pyramids and short columnar trees can be grown in large pots situated on balconies, patios, or in courtyards. Peaches, nectarines, figs, and citrus fruit are all particularly successful in containers.

Pruning fruit trees is magical, in that you can greatly affect the shape and fruitfulness by a few simple cuts, but any mystique attached to it is unwarranted. In fact, too much pruning of mature trees promotes large amounts of new growth that need more pruning, so less is usually more.

Buying fruit trees

A tree can be bought as a one-year-old (maiden), which is just a single stem or with a few sideshoots (feathered maiden). It will need shaping over a few years to make a good framework. Trees that are three or four years old will be more expensive, but have the advantage of having been already trained into their basic shape. Trees older than this may be slower to establish themselves.

The widest selection is available in fall or late winter. Trees will be either container-grown or bare-rooted.

A container-grown tree should be firm in the pot with a good rootball—lift it by the base of the trunk to check. A split container could mean a dry rootball because water may have run out rather than soaked in. Small white roots growing through the bottom of the pot are fine, but more sturdy growth can mean that it has outgrown the pot and has not had enough nourishment.

Bare-rooted trees should be bought while dormant, in winter and very early spring. They will either have their roots wrapped in burlap or plastic or be potted in containers (described as containerized, not container-grown). Check for a straight trunk, strong branches with evenly spaced buds and a balanced root system spreading in all directions. The soil around the roots should be damp and there should be no white roots growing into the soil, which would mean the tree is no longer dormant.

A Medlar?

Some wonderful old-fashioned fruits are often less trouble than "everyday" fruits but sometimes get overlooked. Medlars and quinces have eye-catching blossoms and a heavenly scent. Gages, both green and golden, make a change from ordinary plums, as do damsons, which actually thrive on a poor soil. Mulberries are slow growing but are beautiful trees with historical appeal.

The right tree?
♦ choose suitable rootstock for the size of tree you want.
♦ choose a variety that will give you what you want: for eating or cooking, early, mid-season or late, to eat right away or to store. There are many more varieties than appear in stores. Try as many as you can, or ask an expert for a recommendation.
♦ if planting several trees, choose a mixture that will cross-pollinate and provide fruit over a long period.
♦ check on pollination requirements before buying (see the box below).

On all trees, check the graft union, the knobbly bit near the base of the trunk. It should be free from cracks. Avoid a tree with shoots growing below the union—a bad sign meaning that the graft has not taken completely. If you buy in spring, check that the roots haven't dried out or that the branches haven't been knocked off. Broken branches are not an irreversible problem but are a site for disease and cutting them out may affect the shape. There should be no visible pests.

How to plant

Fruit trees need all the best things, such as deep, fertile soil, good drainage, sun, and shelter. They also prefer a slightly acid soil at least 2 feet (60cm) deep. Cherries require 3 feet (90cm) of good soil.

For making a small orchard, rototill the area and mulch heavily around the trees to inhibit regrowth of grass that can compete for nutrients and moisture. Plant rows north to south to gain maximum light. Keeping the soil grass-free also gives the chance to sow some wild flowers (or they may appear of their own accord), which will attract pollinating insects. Once established, trees will happily grow with grass right up to the trunk.

Trees in containers can be planted any time because the rootball is developed within the pot, but fall is ideal. Plant bare-rooted trees in fall or early spring, and the earlier the better during this time. If the trees have to wait more than several days for planting because the ground is too wet, "heel" them in. Dig a shallow hole or trench, lay the roots in with the tree trunks at an oblique angle, mound soil over the top and firm down. If there is danger of frost, spread straw or plastic over the soil. Trees can be stored like this for a month or more but don't use it as an excuse not to plant them because they will be much happier upright and settling into their permanent positions. If the ground is frozen, store trees in a cool but frost-proof place with the roots covered. Soak dry roots in a bucket for two hours before planting.

Pollination
Some trees (like Victoria plums) are self-fertile, meaning they set fruits with their own pollen, but many require another tree nearby with which to cross-pollinate, and even self-fertile cultivars produce heavier crops if cross-pollinated. Trees in neighboring gardens will do the job if they are not too far away and can be guaranteed to blossom at the same time.

Planting a fruit tree

For planting, dig a hole wide enough to hold the outspread roots (with a semi-standard tree this will be approximately 2 feet and with a bush tree approximately 18 inches). Dig it deep enough for the taproot (the central root beneath the mark where the soil came to when the tree was planted before) to sit comfortably in the hole with the old soil mark level with the ground. There also needs to be room for spreading a 4–6 inch layer of bulky organic material across the base of the hole. For semi-standards the depth will be approximately 2 feet deep and for bush trees, 12–18 inches. The tap root can go down into the organic material and, if necessary, can be trimmed to fit if it is too long. Cut back any other long roots to 12 inches.

Although a tree is planted with the soil mark from the nursery at the same level, check that this mark is not at or above the graft union where the tree was grafted onto the rootstock. The soilmark should be about 4 inches below the join. If a tree is planted above the join, shoots will emerge from the rootstock rather than from the cultivar you have bought.

Loosen the soil at the bottom of the hole with a fork and fork in bulky, well-rotted garden compost or manure. Offer the tree up to measure the roots and put the stake on the windward side. The stake should go 2 feet into the ground and be as tall as the trunk before the first branches start. Put the tree gently to one side (cover roots with plastic so they don't dry out). Take the stake and hammer it so that it's just firm in the hole. Pick up the tree and hold it in the hole at the right depth against the stake. A helper is useful at this point but if there is no one, lean the tree against the stake and fill a little soil into the hole. Pull the tree upright, shake down the soil, and fill in a little more until the roots are covered and you can tread the earth down. Take care when treading to firm the soil that you do not put your whole weight down and break the roots. The tree should be firm without holding and closely in line with the stake. The closer it is to the stake, the less it will move later on. Stand back to check that both tree and stake are vertical. Fill the rest of the hole with earth, and firm it so that once the ground is level again, the soil mark is still just visible. Planting slightly high will allow you to place a thick weed-suppressing, moisture-retaining mulch around the tree.

Staking a fruit tree

Use tree ties to tie the tree to the stake with a spacer so that the bark isn't rubbed. Tie it firmly and loosen it as the trunk grows in subsequent years. For low stakes see page 68.

For planting a container-grown tree, put the stake in at an angle on the side away from the prevailing wind, so that it misses the rootball and bolsters the plant from being blown. Lightly loosen the rootball at the base when it is in the hole.

Once established, trees that have had a good start in life will require only a top dressing of general fertilizer every three years in early spring.

Training a young fruit tree

To prune an apple or pear tree as an open vase-shape between Nov–Feb:

Year 1 After planting a maiden whip, cut the single-stemmed leader back to 30 inches for a bush or 4 feet for a half-standard, just above a bud to stimulate lateral growth.

Year 2 Select four of the branches which have formed. These should be the strongest and the best placed for forming the sides of a wide circular bowl around the trunk. Remove other ones that are not needed (there will only be one or two). Prune back vigorous branches by half and less vigorous ones by two-thirds. Cut to outward facing buds.

Year 3 At the end of the third year's growth, secondary branches will have formed and more laterals will have sprouted from lower down on the original four branches which will also have leaders growing from the top. Select another four branches to continue the framework with the first four. Cut out any others that are not part of this framework at their base. Prune all leaders, vigorous ones by half and less vigorous ones by two-thirds. Cut to outward facing buds. In the center of the tree, prune inward growing laterals back to four buds which will encourage fruit spurs to develop. On the outside of the tree leave laterals that are growing outward unless they are too long, in which case cut them back in proportion with the tree and to strengthen them.

Year 4 By now the framework has been formed and pruning is to encourage fruit. For one more year, cut back vigorous leaders by one-half and less vigorous ones by two-thirds. In subsequent years restrict leader pruning to misplaced branches growing inward, diseased or damaged ones, or weak ones. More pruning will encourage growth rather than fruit. Prune back inner laterals to four buds to encourage spurs on which fruit will form. Leave laterals on the outside unpruned.

Restricted shapes

Fruit trees trained into one of a range of flat shapes have advantages over traditional "tree" shapes in certain situations. They can be trained either against a fence or wall or tied into wires between posts.

For these shapes, build the support first using heavy-gauge galvanized wires. Space posts 8–12 feet apart and for cordons and espaliers, space the wires at 18 inches.

Attach to walls with vine eyes to secure wires firmly. Set at 4 foot (120cm) intervals, leaving at least 3 inches between the wires and the wall. When planting against a wall, plant at least 9 inches (22cm) away from the wall to avoid the dry soil at its base and add extra organic matter to retain moisture in this notoriously dry situation. Feed annually in early spring.

To prune a cordon apple or pear:

Year 1 (Nov–Feb) Plant the maiden with the scion uppermost against a cane at 45 degrees which is attached to the wire supports. Tie the main stem to the cane with soft string. Prune all laterals to four buds.

Year 1 (following Nov) Prune laterals to 4 buds and sub-laterals to 1 or 2 buds.

Year 2 (spring) Cut off flowers carefully —without damaging the leaves—to prevent fruit from forming.

Year 2 (summer, mid-July–Sept) Cut laterals above the 3rd leaf above the basal cluster. On lateral side-shoots, cut above the first leaf above the basal cluster.

Year 3 and subsequent years (mid-July –early August) Continue to prune laterals to three leaves above the basal cluster and the sub-laterals to one leaf above the basal cluster, or 1 inch from the stem. When the leader has passed the top wire (7 feet) cut it back in May and repeat each year to within 1/2 inch of old wood. In winter thin over-crowded spur

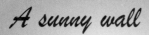

A sunny wall

Don't let a sheltered, sunny wall go to waste. This is just the place for a wall-trained fig, peach, or nectarine.

systems by removing weak buds, overlapping ones, and those on the shady or underside of the cordon.

To prune an apple or pear espalier:

Year 1 (Nov–Feb) Plant a single-stemmed maiden. Cut it back to within 15 inches of the ground. Make the cut above a short leg and three good buds, the lower two pointing in opposite directions.

Year 2 (spring) Direct the shoot from the top bud vertically upward and the side buds to the right and the left.

Year 2 (June–Sept) Continue to train the central shoot upward by attaching a cane to the wires. Attach two other canes to the wires at angles of 45 degrees, so the lower right and left shoots can be trained along it.

Year 2 (Nov) Take away the two angled canes and lower the side branches to the horizontal and tie them carefully in to the lowest wire. Prune them back by one-third to a downward facing bud. Cut back the central leader to within 18 inches of the lower branches above three good buds which will form a new central leader and two new horizontal branches. Cut back surplus laterals on the main stem to three buds, both above and below the first tier.

Year 3 (July–Sept) Repeat year 2 but also cut back competing growths on the main stem to three leaves and laterals on the horizontal branches to three leaves above basal clusters.

Protection

Where rabbits are a nuisance, fruit trees will need spiral or mesh guards 3 feet (1m) high. Stouter and more permanent protection will be needed against deer.

Cherries are a favorite with birds, who will damage the blossoms in spring and the fruit in summer. Use netting over the whole tree if possible or around the sides of a large tree.

Trees in an exposed, windy area may need temporary windbreaks for the first couple of years. These could be plastic mesh attached to strong posts, wooden fencing or even bales of straw or hay.

Pruning

Fruit trees are first pruned in order to train them to the shape required, and then to encourage fruit and maintain the tree's health. Continued pruning is especially necessary for restricted shapes. (For specific pruning advice, see pages 118–119 and page 121.)

Winter pruning for apples and pears

Avoid a frosty day since frost can encourage disease to enter the pruning cuts. Do not prune stone fruit (cherries and plums and their gage and damson relations) now.

Young trees Follow pruning pattern shown on page 118.

Established trees Cut back laterals (sideshoots) on the inside to 4 inches (10cm) and leave the growth on the outside. Where flowerbuds have formed on unpruned laterals, cut them back to make the tree more compact and stronger.

Restricted shapes Cut back laterals of cordons as described on page 119. Thin overcrowded spur systems on established plants by removing weak buds, overlapping ones, and those on the shady or underside of the cordon. On espaliers, lower the side branches to the horizontal, tie them, and prune back.

Spring pruning

Restricted shapes Carefully cut flowers off first-year trees to prevent fruit forming. Tie espalier-trained branches as described on page 119. When the leader of an espalier has passed the top wire, cut it back each year in late spring. On mature trees, cut horizontals back to fit their space (see page 119).

Summer pruning

Restricted shapes Cut back cordon laterals as as described on page 119. Continue to tie lengthening stems of espaliers and fans.

Stone fruit Carry out pruning of cherries, plums, and their relations before the end of the summer in order to avoid silver leaf disease, which is more likely to take hold when the trees are dormant in winter.

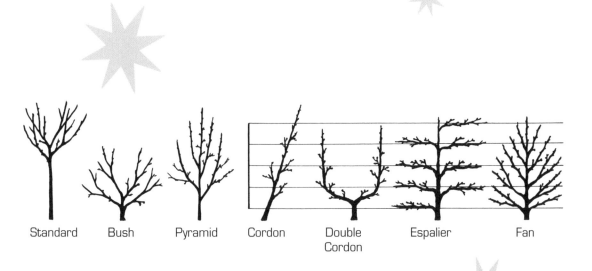

Standard   Bush   Pyramid   Cordon   Double Cordon   Espalier   Fan

A pyramid-shaped apple tree in a pot
Buy a two-year-old plant and choose a large container, 12–15 inches (30–40cm) in diameter. Ensure good drainage (see page 134), fill with good-quality multi-purpose compost and add a stake for support. Water daily in hot, dry weather and protect from heavy frosts by wrapping the pot or moving it indoors to a cool but frost-proof place.

In winter cut the main leader back by half, the upper branches by two-thirds and the lower by one-third. Cut weak branches and those not necessary for making a conical shape. Remove the top 1–2 inches (3–5cm) of compost and replace with nutrient-rich garden compost.

The following summer cut back the leader by one-third to a bud on the opposite side from the winter pruning direction. This keeps the main stem vertical. Prune all the other branches back by one-third and again take out any weak or ill-placed branches. Give a liquid high-potash feed every two weeks when the fruits start to swell and a nitrogen-rich fertilizer in late summer. Repot every two years at the end of the winter.

chapter 4 *The Space*

Any garden is a mixture of mini-environments. Even a pocket handkerchief plot can have ground cover thriving in the shade of taller plants, flowers attracting insects that will feed on pests and pollinate other flowers, and a wall or fence that shields the garden from the wind and gives support for climbers. Given a little more room to play with, shrubs and trees will give more support, shade, and flowers, as well as providing a home for birds and more insects. A lawn will attract its own mini-wildlife and create a calm green foil to the busier textures of flowers and leaves, and be somewhere to relax and for children to play. Water adds yet another dimension, bringing reflective light and sound to a garden and providing a habitat for different plants and wildlife.

Containers are miniature garden environments in themselves. Mobile and versatile, they both enhance and increase the planting space. Rooftop gardens expand garden space and can be highly rewarding if planted to suit the conditions.

Lawns and meadows

It is perhaps the expectation of a perfectly smooth expanse of green that makes lawns potentially labor-intensive and their owners sometimes obsessive. In reaction, some gardeners do away with a lawn altogether. But paving or planting cannot supply the calming, springy greenness of grass, and in winter it is uplifting to see all the muted russets, browns, and parchment set against a carpet of green. In creating or caring for a lawn, decide on its function. The types of grass will affect its texture and its wearability.

Mmm, that grass smells good

Sweet-scented chamomile: is good in warm climates. Softer and springier than grass, but shorter lived and can produce bare patches and turn brown in winter. The non-flowering dwarf *Anthemis nobilis* "Treneague" is best. Use in a free-draining, sunny spot.

Creeping thyme (*Thymus serpyllum*): is also sweetly scented but can become thin and uneven, so limit to a small area. Likes the same conditions as chamomile. Paths sown with Pennyroyal *(Mentha pulegium)* or Corsican mint *(M. requienii)* will give a lovely aroma when walked on. Can be invasive, so provide a barrier edging.

Velvety lawn	Fine-leaved grasses like tuft-forming *Festuca* varieties and creeping bent grasses (*Agrostis*)	Won't stand up to heavy wear or neglect and needs regular close mowing to prevent tougher grasses gaining a hold. Coarse weeds are noticeable. Bumps and hollows also stand out, but this makes it good for making sculptural contours.
Hardwearing everyday lawn	Broadleaved meadow or perennial rye grasses (*Lolium perenne*) with tall fescue (*festuca* spp.) or zoysia (*zoysia*).	Less expensive as both turf and seed, and quick growing. Needs frequent cutting in spring and summer, but will tolerate heavy use and neglect. Self-seeding wild grasses soon become a part of the lawn.
Rough grass areas	Fine and broadleaved varieties with Kentucky blue grass (*Poa pratense*). Also perennial rye grass (*Lolium perenne*) and meadow foxtail (*Alopecauris pratensis*).	Low maintenance, cutting twice a year (see Meadows, page 130). Poor contrast to flower borders, but good for a wild area, with wild flowers and naturalized bulbs. Attracts insects and butterflies.

A new lawn

Sod or seed? Each has its advantages and disadvantages.

Sod (Turf)	Seed
♦ gives instant cover and color	♦ much cheaper than sod
♦ can be walked on soon after laying	♦ sowing takes less effort than manoeuvring
♦ preparing the soil doesn't have to be so	heavy sod pieces
thorough	♦ can be stored until conditions are right
♦ not damaged by birds	♦ won't introduce weeds once you have
but	prepared the ground
♦ more expensive, especially for top quality	**but**
grasses	♦ takes a year to reach maturity, during
♦ deteriorates quickly if not laid soon after	which time it needs careful attention
delivery	♦ seed needs protecting from birds
♦ may contain coarse grasses and weeds.	♦ seedlings are vulnerable to damping off,
	drought and competition from weeds.

The best time for sowing is from late summer to early fall or else in mid-spring. Sod is best laid during fall or winter, but it can also be put down in early spring. Ground preparation, however, should begin one to three months in advance.

Start by clearing the site of all greenery and debris. Decide on levels. A gentle slope is not a problem but abrupt irregularities need to be smoothed out—a step or terrace to change levels can become a feature. Improve soil texture and drainage by adding bulky organic matter or gritty sand. On a plot prone to water-logging drains may be needed (see page 26).

Dig the area, taking out perennial weeds and stones. If rototilling, go over the ground once a month for three months to help eradicate weeds that divide and regrow.

A couple of weeks before you are ready to sow or lay sod, turn the roughly dug area into a firm, level bed. The soil should not be too wet or it will prove a muddy, backbreaking task. Break down the clods of turned earth with a roller or, alternatively, by trampling them. Rake the soil, removing more stones and debris that will have come to the surface. A week later, firm the ground by shuffling over it, steps close together and your weight on your heels. Rake even and repeat the operation at right angles to the first way you walked. Rake again and repeat until there are no uneven patches or bumps. Finally, rake a slow-release general fertilizer (one handful per square yard or meter) into the surface and leave the soil to settle for another week.

Now I get the chance to test drive this little beauty!

Laying sod (turf)

Buy sod from a reputable supplier. It should have a uniform healthy growth without visible weeds and with good root growth. Sod is rolled with the grass inward for transporting. If you are not able to lay it immediately unroll it in a shady spot with the grass upward and water.

1 Lay the first row along one side, overhanging the edge slightly. Remove weeds in the sod as you see them and discard any that are too bare of grass. If an unevenness appears as you lay the sod, add or scrape away soil to level it.

2 Firm down the first row by laying planks over it and walking on them, then work from the planks to lay the next row.

3 Stagger joins like brickwork and overlay all the outer edges. Cut sod to fit round curves rather than pulling or stretching it.

4 Trim outer edges with a flat-bladed spade. Fill small gaps with multi-purpose compost.

5 Gently brush the laid lawn with a stiff broom or a leaf rake to lift flattened grass and remove any debris. Water thoroughly with a spray hose or sprinkler.

Until the new lawn is established, it will need watering when the weather is dry. Should cracks from shrinkage appear, fill with compost or soil as before. When growth starts in spring, mow first with the blades set high and gradually lower them as the lawn becomes more established.

Sowing seed

Buy a seed mix according to your requirements (see page 123). Or have fun and experiment with your own mix.

1 Choose a dry, still day when the top of the soil is dry but underneath it is moist. Give the surface a final rake (a seed-sown lawn needs an even finer tilth than sod).

2 Shake or mix the seed in its container to mix the varieties thoroughly. Sow according to instructions on the packet or at about one small handful per square yard or meter.

3 A push seeder will help give even distribution. Otherwise, mark out strips about a yard or meter wide. Divide the seed in half and divide one half into the number of strips. Sow each strip with its allocated pile of seed.

4 Mark out new strips at right angles to the first ones and sow the other half of the seed in the same way.

5 Rake the seed lightly into the soil. Most seed is treated with a bird repellant. If it isn't, criss-cross a web of cotton thread over the area. Water with a very fine, gentle spray.

Grass seed takes one to three weeks to germinate depending on weather. Don't let it dry out, but don't overwater.

When the new grass is about 1¹/₂ inches (4cm) high, sweep worm casts and debris away and roll with a light roller to firm the soil

Be kind

Before mowing, check there are no small animals like frogs hiding in the grass.

and to encourage deeper rooting. After a few days, sweep again and mow with the blades set high. Gradually lessen the height of the mower blades until the lawn is mowed regularly at ³/₄–1¹/₄ inches (2–3cm). Weed newly sown lawns carefully to avoid uprooting young grasses.

Mowing

Regular mowing encourages a thick, firm, resiliant lawn that will crowd out weeds and moss and be resistant to drought. Grass grows much more slowly in winter, and a lawn will survive winter better if it is left slightly long. Longer grass survives drought and cold better. Between these weather extremes, mowing depends on the rate of growth. In spring a weekly mowing is enough but during late spring and summer, play areas and neater lawns will benefit from a twice-weekly cut. Most lawns are best kept at about ³/₄–1¹/₄ inches (2–3cm) in summer. Fine-quality lawns can be cut a little closer but be careful to not scrape areas bare. Avoid cutting

very wet grass, and tackle very long grass in stages, setting the mower at its highest cut.

Tools for lawns

Lawnmower: what you choose will depend on the size and type of lawn, and your budget. A cylinder mower will provide a finer finish than a rotary mower but copes less well with overgrown grass and rough or wet conditions. For a very small area, a hand-powered mower may be all you need, and will save you the trouble and expense of fuel or the worry of electric cables.

Long-handled shears: to trim edges or around trees.

Strimmer or brushcutter: requires less effort than shears and can deal with rougher grass but leaves a less neat effect.

Lawn rake: for scarifying (see page 128) and clearing leaves.

Feeding and maintaining

Rake worm casts and debris off the lawn in early spring and scatter a general fertilizer such as blood, fish, and bone or a proprietary organic lawn fertilizer. Garden compost can also be spread thinly across the lawn if you have enough to spare. If the lawn looks green and is growing well, there is no need to feed it annually, but a dressing of kelp meal or a watering with liquid seaweed can improve a tired lawn. If growth is still poor, feed again in summer and apply a dressing to improve soil structure (see box) in autumn. An easy rule of thumb is: feed in spring and improve soil in autumn.

Thatch—a build-up of matted fibrous material and dead grass—prevents water from reaching the soil, encourages diseases, and stops grass from thickening up. Remove it by raking vigorously with a metal-tined rake (scarifying). Also rake out moss, which thrives where drainage is poor. Scarify in early autumn when grass will still be able to produce sideshoots to thicken up, and seed any large bare patches.

Acid conditions encourage thatch and moss. If the pH is below 7, apply an annual dressing of lime, either as ground limestone or dolomitic lime. Sprinkle it across the lawn and gently brush or rake it in.

Aerating a lawn improves air and water absorption. This is only necessary for compacted soils and does not need to be done more than once in every three years unless the problem is serious, in which case scarifying and top dressing to improve soil structure will also help. A fork with hollow tines, which takes out a core of soil about 4 inches (10cm) long, is better than an ordinary fork, which will allow some air and drainage but increases compaction around the holes. Brush sand into the holes.

Top dressing to improve soil structure for lawns

For heavy soils:
3 parts sharp sand
1 part sterilized topsoil (loam)
1 part bulky organic material (2-year-old leafmold, composted municipal green waste, or composted shredded bark)

For light soils:
2 parts sterilized topsoil
3 parts bulky organic material

To increase fertility, choose a high-fertility organic material or mix in fertilizer. Apply dressing thinly to avoid stifling grass growth.

Sweeping

A natural twig broom is good for brushing in top dressings. Buy one or make your own from birch or broom twigs.

Renovating a neglected lawn

• Cut overlong grass in stages, with either a rotary mower on its highest setting or a string trimmer, and rake up.

• Continue to cut and rake until the grass is down to about 2 inches (5cm) in height, then mow at least once a week through the summer. Leave short cuttings as a mulch.

• Dig out large weeds.

• Rake to remove stones, dead grass and debris.

• Feed (see page 128) in spring or summer.

• Fill holes and hollows with garden compost and sprinkle grass seed over them. Keep these patches well watered.

• Lime an acid soil (see pages 11–12).

• Aerate waterlogged areas, pushing a hollow-tined fork down 6–8 inches (15–20cm) and fill holes with sharp sand or grit.

Some indicators of lawn problems

• Moss may mean the site is too dark and damp. Reduce the shade if you can, or choose an alternative groundcover.

• Daisies are more numerous on compacted soils and lawns that are cut very short.

• Clover grows well on poor soils; feeding will help to deter it.

• Sheep's sorrel (*Rumex acetosella*) is an indicator of acid conditions

• Plantain and thistles grow where grass is thin or patchy. Weed, aerate, feed, and re-seed.

Wild flower meadows and lazy mowing

Rough grass and wild flowers attracts bees, butterflies, and other wildlife. You could simply leave an area of grass uncut and see what appears. Both grasses and flowers will grow and set seed. If you never cut it, tougher shrubby plants will begin to invade. To encourage spring flowers, cut or mow after midsummer; for summer meadows, cut in early fall and mow in spring. Cut during dry weather and leave the cuttings on the surface for two or three days to release their ripe seeds, then rake up and compost (taking the cuttings away helps reduce soil fertility). Although wild flowers would not mind fertile soil, it encourages the tougher grasses, docks, and nettles, which push out the wild flowers. In poor soil the grasses don't grow as well but the wild flowers will flourish.

Sowing a wild flower meadow

Remove the topsoil or dig, turning it under the poorer subsoil. Rake and firm as if you were preparing a lawn. Leave for a few weeks for the first flush of weeds to appear, and hoe them off. Broadcast your wild flower mix over the surface and rake in gently. Or plant plugs of wild flowers. Establish your new meadow in spring and keep it watered until the seeds have germinated and the meadow has established itself.

Crocuses, snowdrops, snake's head fritillaries, and dwarf narcissi all add spring color to a meadow. After flowering leave at least six weeks before cutting, to allow the goodness in the leaves to transfer to the bulb for next year. Trim the grass in late fall so that the bulbs aren't lost in long grass in the spring.

Lazy mowing

Lazy mowing —simply mowing grass paths through rough grass—can be both practical and attractive. The mown paths make a contrasting frame to the long, waving grasses and seedheads, and it is quicker to mow a path than a whole lawn. The paths can meander like a pleasant walk or provide direct access to another part of the garden.

Making a Pond with a Butyl Liner

1 Mark out the shape of the pond with a piece of string or rope. Plan a shallow shelf for growing marginal plants and make sure that there is at least one edge which slopes gently down from the surface. This forms a safe access route for amphibious wildlife to climb in and out of the pond. The deepest part of the pond needs to be at least 24in deep to protect pondlife from frost in winter and to keep cool in summer.

2 Butyl is the strongest of the plastic liners and can last for 40 to 50 years. To find the amount needed, measure the maximum length and maximum width of the pond, and add twice the maximum depth to each of these figures. The resultant figures give the size of liner (eg. max. length. 9ft max. width 4ft, max depth 3ft requires a liner of 15ft x 10ft).

3 Take the sod off and set to one side. Dig the hole for the pond larger than the planned size by about 6in: Dig sloping rather than vertical sides down to the deepest point. Cut out shallow water areas as shelves about 12in wide and 9–12in deep with a horizontal base for pots to sit on. If the pond is to be viewed from the house make sure the shelf margins which may have tall iris or reeds growing on them do not block the view of the water.

4 Remove all sharp stones, roots, and anything which might puncture the liner. Firm the sides and surface as evenly as possible. Smooth a 4in layer of damp builder's sand around the inside surface of the hole and follow this with another protective layer of old carpet, cardboard, or a proprietary brand of pond underlay.

5 With assistance (butyl liners are heavy), lay the liner over the hole with a 12in overlap around the edges and let it dip halfway down into the lowest depth. Put heavy stones to weigh down the edges. A repeat of the outside protective layer inside the liner will further protect the liner if you have to step inside the pond at any stage and cover the base with low fertility soil if you are going to plant directly into it.

6 Fill the pond with either rainwater or tap water. For tap water, wait 48 hours after filling for the chlorine to dissipate before planting oxygenating plants. The weight of water will mold the liner to the depth and shape of the pond. Bury the edges under sod (set to one side from the excavation) or under earth, gravel and/or stones so that the surface of the liner is protected from light which will make it brittle. Pond edges can also be covered with stone slabs which slightly overhang the edges. Similarly, keep the pool filled with water to prevent deterioration of the liner.

Water

A natural source of water in your garden is a wonderful asset, but it can also be very satisfying to create your own, whether it's a wildlife pond, a formal reflecting pool, or just a bubble fountain.

Water encourages wildlife. Birds will come to drink and bathe in the smallest receptacle of fresh water, and other animals will also lap at the edges if the approach is easy. Pondlife appears without having to do anything about it. Even fish will appear without being introduced, as spawn is carried by birds or over land and dropped into the pond. This is part of the magic of ponds.

For a pond to naturalize, it needs to have both light and shade. To be good for wildlife it requires a gentle sloping side to allow access for small creatures and a deeper area, at least 2 feet (60cm), that will be frost-free in winter and cool in summer. A range of different depths will increase the variety of plants that will grow.

Pond plants

Water plants can be classed as marginals, aquatics, and oxygenators.

Marginals

Marginals prefer no more than 2–3 inches (5–7cm) of water over their roots. Plant them in mesh baskets into a medium loam with a half-handful of bonemeal and cover the surface with gravel to discourage fish from stirring it up. Either sit the baskets on a pond shelf or, in deeper water, stand them on a brick plinth.

- **Marsh marigold** (*Caltha palustris*). Spring flowers like oversize buttercups.
- **Water poppy** (*Hydrocleys nymphoides*). Sunny yellow flowers.
- **Flag iris** (*Iris pseudacorus*). Yellow flowers.
- **Water mint** (*Mentha aquatica*). Aromatic pink flowers, good for butterflies.
- **Pickerel weed** (*Pontederia cordata*).Pretty blue spires.
- **Bog bean** (*Menyanthes trifoliata*). White flowers.

Aquatics

Aquatics grow in deeper water. Plant them up like marginals, and introduce them in stages to deep water.

- **Waterlilies** (*Nymphaea*). Some have a huge spread, so check which are suitable for the size of your pond.
- **Water hawthorn** (*Aponogeton distachyos*). Curiously-shaped, fragrant spring flowers.
- **Water hyacinth** (*Eichhornia crassipes*). A subtropical aquatic that floats on the surface. Pretty for its scented lilac flowers.
- **Frogbit** (*Hydrocharis* spp.) Floating perennial with white flowers.

Oxygenators

Oxygenating plants are added to maintain healthy water. Weight them down with lead and let them sink to the deepest part of the pond.

- **Hornwort** (*Ceratophyllum demersum* and *C. submersum*)
- **Water milfoil** (*Myriophyllum spicatum* and *M. verticillatum*)
- **Water starworts** (*Callitriche stagnalis*)
- **Curly pondweed** (*Petamogeton crispus*)

Containers

Containers add variety and versatility to gardens large and small. They introduce new shapes and colors, bring herbs to the kitchen door, and can be moved around and replanted for fresh interest all year. Containers allow you to grow plants where there is no soil and to achieve plant combinations that would not work in the open garden.

Choosing a container

Plants will grow in anything from antique terracotta pots to a tin with holes punched in the bottom—all they need is suitable soil, room for their roots, and sufficient drainage. So choosing a container is largely an aesthetic matter. Some points to consider:

♦ **Terracotta pots** may crack in winter if they are not frost-proof.
♦ **"Olive jar" pots** are an attractive shape but don't use them for plants that will need potting on as it is almost impossible to get a large plant through the narrow neck without damage.
♦ **Clay pots** are more expensive than plastic, but their porosity allows air to reach roots and moisture to evaporate. Glazed clay looks good when the plants have been chosen to complement the pot's color.
♦ **Plastic pots** need less watering, are easier to clean, and usually have better drainage.
♦ **Oak, cedar, and sweet chestnut** are naturally resistant to rot, but less durable woods will need to be painted, varnished, or charred inside to prevent decay.

Aging pots

Containers made of cement or reconstituted stone are much cheaper than real stone, but can look very raw. Accelerate the aging process by coating the sides with yogurt or manure.

♦ **Galvanized metal containers** will not rust but recycled tin cans, such as paint pots, will. Paint to delay rusting and don't forget to pierce drainage holes in the bottom.
♦ **Window boxes** should be at least 9 inches (23cm) deep; stand on a drip tray to avoid nutrient-rich water staining the wall below.

Planting

Fill the bottom of pots with gravel or broken crocks (make this a fifth of the total height in stone or terracotta pots if it is likely to freeze in winter). To give weight to light containers, add small stones. Use broken-up polystyrene packaging to limit the weight of heavy containers. Stand pots on bricks or pottery feet to improve drainage further and move large containers into place before filling.

A good-quality multi-purpose compost works well for most plants, or you can make your own (see page 34). For plants that like dry situations, such as pelargoniums and lavender, add more sand. Add coir (see page 15) or use ericaceous compost for acid-loving plants and add lime (see pages 11–12) for clematis and other lime lovers.

Aftercare

Plants in containers can't stretch out their roots to seek moisture and sustenance. Plants under stress will be weaker and more susceptible to pests like red spider mite, aphids, or whitefly, so try to get in the habit of checking them regularly.

Many will need watering daily in summer but not often in autumn or winter—push your finger into the soil to see what conditions are like below the surface. If the compost does dry out, put any containers that are not too large in basins of water to take up water slowly from the base. Water large pots under the foliage, directing water at the roots.

In spring give a top dressing of a slow-release fertilizer like blood, fish, and bone, kelp meal, or your own well-rotted garden compost. Requirements then vary: a slow-growing shrub will need nothing more, but a crowded tub or basket of annuals will benefit from weekly fertilization while in flower (see page 12 for advice on what nutrients are needed when). A soil-improving mulch in autumn will help plants through the winter. Move tender plants into frost-free shelter when necessary.

Slug battles

A wide band of Vaseline round the top of a pot may deter slugs and snails.

Hanging baskets

Taking sphagnum moss from the wild is causing environmental damage, so use other liners available in shops or make your own—old woollen fabric cut to size will hold moisture well. Use a soilless medium for lightness and, because baskets dry out fast, mix in a wetting agent. Plant trailing plants from the base up, through the mesh of wire baskets and around the rim. Water daily and once flowers begin to appear, fertilize weekly with a tomato or other high-potash fertilizer and deadhead regularly.

Roof gardens

A roof garden high above the crowded city streets feels like a retreat from the humdrum or the everyday worries of life.

Planting a roof garden has its own particular problems, but the first question is whether the roof is strong enough. Before embarking on any plans, get expert advice from a structural engineer. It is not only the weight of perhaps several people that needs to be considered, but the surprisingly heavy burden of soil and plants, a suitable surface to walk on and how to avoid dampness from penetrating under the planted containers. You will also need to think about practicalities such as access to water and storage for gardening paraphernalia from plant fertilizer to a trowel. A rooftop environment is exposed to unobstructed sun and wind which can cause leaves to scorch and pots to dry out before midday.

Strategically placed trellis will shelter plants and also provide privacy for you. A bold

beamed pergola across some or all of the roof garden would give strong support to trellising or for climbing plants. Tough shrubs like pyracantha, cotoneaster, and berberis will deflect winds, while climbing roses or slower-growing clematis, winter-flowering jasmine (*Jasminum nudiflorum*), and its fragrant summer-flowering cousin, *J. officinale*, will in time give protection for other plants.

Once you have manipulated this inhospitable environment to give shade and shelter, you can grow any plants that are happy in containers, including food plants and herbs, small trees, grasses, and bulbs. Leave a small space for a deckchair and enjoy your hidden paradise!

Pests and diseases

Lists of pests and diseases are always daunting, because they instill a fear that your garden could be blighted by all of them. Many, however, only flourish in certain conditions or certain localities. For this reason the list below does not extend to possible mammalian nuisances, such as pets, rabbits, moles, and deer. There are some basic deterrent suggestions in the book on some of these, but it is best to get local advice, which will have been tested for your area.

Ants	do not attack plants but feed on honeydew excreted by aphids or scale insects which they protect by farming them. Control: destroy nests with boiling water or pyrethrum-based products as directed; apply grease bands to trees.
Aphids	sap-sucking pests including greenfly, blackfly, and other colors. They colonize leaves, stems, young shoots, and also roots. Control: pick off and squash them; check plant health; encourage natural predators; spray with insecticidal soap; cut off affected tips and destroy.
Cabbage caterpillars	laid by imported cabbage moths. Eat leaves of brassicas, sometimes nasturtiums. Control: squash eggs or pick off caterpillars; avoid by covering crop with floating row covers or fine mesh netting to stop moths landing.
Cabbage root fly	eggs laid near the stems of brassicas produce larvae which tunnel into the roots. Control: grow individual plants and protect when planting out with flat cardboard or felt discs placed on the earth around the base of stems [see page 97].
Canker	fungal disease of apple and pear trees causing bark to shrink and crack. Control: cut out diseased branches.
Carrot rust fly	from late spring, small black flies lay eggs which produce larvae. These tunnel into carrot roots, foliage can redden, and growth is stunted. Control: a barrier around the carrot bed is the most effective.
Cucumber beetle	striped or spotted beetles that feed on squash family plants as well as tomatoes, peppers, and eggplants and often transmit cucumber blight disease. Control: crop rotation: row covers (fleece); spray with pyrethrins.
Cutworms	greyish-black caterpillars feeding at or below ground level at night. Plants wilt or may be cut right through. Control: clear weeds around plants; cultivate infested soil in winter to expose to predators; protect transplants with plastic collars pressed into the ground; allow chickens in.
Damping off	fungal disease affecting seedlings. Control: wash pots and trays before sowing; ensure good ventilation; sow seed later inside or when soil has warmed up outside (see page 99).
Flea beetle	tiny beetles that jump when disturbed. During dry spells in late spring small holes speckle youngest leaves of brassicas, stocks, nasturtiums, and tomatoes. Control: garden hygiene; regular watering; coat cardboard with sticky substance, hold above plant and shake plant gently so that beetles jump and stick to it.
Leaf miners	larvae that feed by tunnelling within leaves, making maze patterns. Control: pick off leaves and destroy.

Mineral deficiencies	usually show in poor growth and discolored leaves. Hard to tell which mineral may be lacking but unless expert advice is required, the best remedy is to spray with liquid seaweed and improve the soil structure (see page 12).
Peach leaf curl	fungal disease attacking peach, almonds, and nectarines in early spring. New leaves twist and thicken with red blisters. Control: cover with row cover (fleece) from mid-winter to mid-spring; pick off diseased leaves and destroy; spray with Bordeaux mixture after leaf fall and again before buds swell in late winter.
Powdery mildew	fungal disease common on dry soils during warm days and cold nights. Plants become coated with a grey-white powder. Control: prune out affected parts, mulch to conserve moisture; avoid overfeeding with nitrogen.
Red spider mite	thrives inside in hot, dry, airless conditions. Leaves begin with a fine speckling, followed by fine webbing, before turning brown and dying. Control: spray plants with water; ensure good airflow; put plants outside in summer.
Rose black spot	fungal disease showing as black spots on leaves. Control: prune out infected leaves and destroy; prune infected stems hard in spring; spray with sulphur.
Rust	fungal disease that appears as orange or brown spots on leaves. Control: cut out infected leaves; cut back stems beyond infection; destroy debris.
Scale insects	tiny sap-feeding pests which settle near veins of leaves and stems and excrete a sticky substance. Soft scale are flat with a dark center spot while hard scale have waxy, dome-shaped shells. Control: pick off when seen; wash infested plants gently with soapy water and repeat weekly until infestation is gone.
Slugs and snails	silvery trails in the morning show where pests feed at night. Leaves, shoots, and even bulbs are destroyed. Control: locate pests at night; bait with saucers of beer, milk or grape juice or attract under planks or half-grapefruits and destroy; surround plants with bran and pick pests out; encourage natural predators (birds, ground beetles); protect individual plants with plastic bottle collars; mulch with gravel; put copper coated tape around pots.
Thrips	during hot summers, leaf surfaces of privet, gladioli, peas, and others, indoors and outside, develop a silvery mottling. Control: garden hygiene; regular watering; spray with neem (derris) or pyrethrins.
Vine weevil	dull, brown-black beetles emerging late spring or early summer, which feed on plants, especially in pots, making irregular holes around the edges of leaves. Control: destroy pests when seen; protect pots with tape smeared with non-drying glue or tanglefoot.
Whitefly	thrives inside and during summer outside. Tiny white flies coat plants and fly up in a cloud when disturbed. Plants become sticky and stunted. Control: ensure good airflow; hang proprietory sticky traps near infected plants.
Winter moths	wingless moths climb fruit trees in winter to lay eggs. In spring, caterpillars hatch and eat leaves and blossom. Control: grease bands around trunks from fall to spring.
Wireworms	pale yellow-brown larvae found in grassland or on newly cleared ground; they attack vegetable roots and some ornamentals. Control: cultivate new or infected land in winter to expose pests to predators; attract pests by burying carrot or potato pieces and then dig up and destroy.

Seasonal Tips

Spring

Lawns: Scarify to remove thatch or moss. Aerate, repair dips, reseed bald areas if necessary, and apply a general fertilizer. Set blades high for the first cut. Sow new lawns in mid-spring.

Flowers: Sow hardy and half-hardy annuals inside, hardening off as the weather improves. Dig over flowerbeds, apply soil conditioners or low-fertility top dressing. As the weather warms, sow hardy annuals outside. When all danger of frost has passed, plant out half-hardy annuals. Water seeds and transplants until established. Weed around established plants and mulch with well-rotted compost. Prepare supports for plants that need them.

Bulbs: Let the leaves die down after flowering. Plant fall-flowering bulbs.

Climbers: In early spring, prune for renewal, tidy and tie stems. Top dress with well-rotted compost and mulch to suppress weeds and conserve moisture.

Trees, shrubs and hedges: Prune roses in early spring and again if late frost catches new growth. Plant container-grown plants in early spring and conifers in mid-spring. Remove winter protection from tender shrubs. Feed and mulch. Check ties and stakes. Trim formal hedges in late spring.

Vegetable and fruit garden: Prepare ground, sow seeds inside for transplanting in late spring, sow later seeds in situ and brassicas and leeks in seedbed. Protect crops from cold and predators.

Summer

Lawns: Mow regularly, lowering the height of the blades, but leave grass longer during dry periods. Feed if growth is poor.

Flowers: Plant out half-hardy annuals and sow biennial seed in late spring/early summer. Weed beds and water, mulch where possible. Liquid-feed bedding displays. Check plant supports.

Bulbs: Lift tulip bulbs and store.

Climbers: Prune non-flowering climbers.

Containers: Liquid-feed hanging baskets weekly and pots according to growth.

Trees, shrubs, and hedges: Prune shrubs that flower before midsummer right after flowering. Trim vigorous and formal hedges, including conifers, in early and late summer.

Vegetable and fruit garden: Sow squash (marrows) *in situ* in early summer, plant out young vegetable plants and transplant brassicas (protecting from pests). Harvest crops regularly. Plant new strawberry bed. Prune trained fruit trees. Prune stone fruit (plums etc). Harvest cherries and berries.

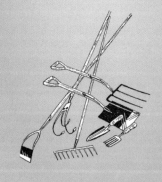

Seasonal Tips

Fall

Lawns: Rake up fallen leaves and compost to use for leafmold or mulch under shrubs. Raise the height of cutting and mow less often. Reseed bald patches. Sow or sod (turf) new lawns.

Flowers: Collect seed, leaving some to self-seed. In early fall, dig heavy soils. Plant out biennials. Divide overlarge plants after flowering. Pot up tender perennials for winter storage before frosts.
In late autumn, tidy borders, cut back perennials, and remove old stems and leaves.

Bulbs: Plant spring-flowering varieties. After frost blackens foliage, dig up dahlia tubers and store. Protect tender bulbs like nerines and gladioli with thick layer of straw or leaves.

Climbers: Plant new climbers. Check established climbers are tied to supports before winter winds catch them.

Containers: Plant up winter pansies. Bring indoors or protect tender plants.

Trees, shrubs, and hedges: Trim hedges for the last time in early autumn. Plant deciduous trees and shrubs, including new hedges.

Vegetable and fruit garden: Prune raspberries, tie new growth. Harvest crops and clear ground for winter. In warm areas, sow winter lettuce and spring cabbages in early fall and broad beans in late fall. Prune apples and pears in late fall/winter.

Winter

Lawns: Apply ground limestone to acidic soil. Service mowers and string trimmers before storing for winter.

Flowers: Order plants and seeds for spring. Check overwintering plants in coldframes or frost-free store once every two weeks for moisture and ventilate when possible.

Bulbs: Check stored tubers after Christmas.

Climbers: Tie back wind-blown plants and, before bud burst, prune those that flowered after midsummer. Feed and mulch.

Containers: Check for frost damage.

Trees and shrubs: In warm climates, plant deciduous varieties during mild spells. Firm shrubs loosened by wind, and stake if necessary.

Vegetable and fruit garden: Dig heavy soils in early winter, light soils in late winter. Apply well-rotted composts and soil conditioners in late winter. Add lime to brassica beds or acid soils. Plant onion sets and shallots. Prune soft fruit bushes. Plant bare-rooted fruit trees.

Index

 *Credits*

Pictures are used courtesy of:

Advertising Archives Ltd: cover, pages 6, 9, 33, 39, 44, 47, 52, 83, 88, 103, 121, 122, 127, 129, 137

Getty Images: pages 13, 19, 20, 25, 29, 30, 41, 48, 55, 57, 61, 64, 69, 72, 77, 90, 95, 105, 108, 111, 112, 114, 117, 131, 135